# COPING
### WITH

# Family
# Stress

**Kimberly Wood Gooden**

ROSEN PUBLISHING GROUP, INC./NEW YORK

Published in 1989 by The Rosen Publishing Group, Inc.

29 East 21st Street, New York, NY 10010

*First Edition*

Library of Congress Cataloging-In-Publication Data

Gooden, Kimberly Wood.
  Coping with family stress / Kimberly Wood
Gooden.—1st ed.
      p.    cm.
  Includes index.
  Summary: Offers guidelines and suggestions for
coping with stressful family situations such as death,
divorce, remarriage, and suicide.
  ISBN 0-8239-0980-8 :
  1. Teenagers—United States—Life skills guides—
Juvenile literature.   2. Children—United States—
Life skills guides—Juvenile literature.   3. Life
change events—United States—Juvenile liter-
ature.   4. Problem families—United States—Juve-
nile literature   [1. Family problems.]   I. Title.
HQ796.G643   1989
158'.24—dc19                                    88-36488
                                                   CIP
                                                   AC

Manufactured in the United States of America

*In loving memory of my lovely little sister*

*Holly Minka Wood*

*Thank you for showing me what is really important in life. You will always live in my heart.*

# A B O U T   T H E   A U T H O R ◇

**A** graduate of the University of Texas, Kimberly Wood Gooden holds a degree in psychology and elementary education. She has been an elementary school teacher for the past eight years in Odessa, Texas.

She has been actively involved in the Compassionate Friends national organization for five years, counseling those who have lost siblings to death.

Mrs. Wood Gooden is a member of Texas Night Writers, Romance Writers of America, and the Society of Children's Book Writers. She has had numerous articles published in national magazines.

# Contents

# CHAPTER 1

# Just Between You and Your Parents

The most important relationship you will ever have during your lifetime is the one between you and your parents. This vital relationship starts the day you are born and follows you whatever path you may take. How you view your parents and how your parents view you shapes your opinions, attitudes, and dreams.

What do you expect from them as parents? What do they expect from you as a child? Can you talk with them as friends? Or is your relationship strictly controlled? Do you feel close to them? Or do you feel like a visitor living in a hotel with them?

Answering these questions honestly can tell you where you stand with your parents. No two families are alike. Every family has its problems as does your family.

But my family and my parents are different, you say. Maybe your parents are separated or divorced. Maybe you don't even live with your natural parents, but with someone else. Maybe you have a stepfather or stepmother.

Whatever your own situation, whatever your feelings may be, reading this chapter can help you. It can help you understand yourself and your parents.

Life is not easy, and nobody ever said it would be. Life can be very stressful. But you can learn to handle your family problems and come out a winner. Remember, you are not alone struggling with family relationships, but it is up to you and only you to maintain a positive and healthy attitude toward a very important part of your life. That is between you and your parents.

Life along with nature is a cycle. It can be called a learning cycle. A cycle is a complete set of events that keep repeating in the same order, such as the cycle of the four seasons. And so it is a cycle you encounter growing up with your parents.

A form of cycle is called bonding. The parent-child relationship has three phases: (1) bonding; (2) detachment; and (3) reunion. When each phase begins and ends depends on the unique circumstances of each family. The phases require parental intuition about when to ease into the debonding period or detachment and come together in the reunion stage. How well do your parents acknowledge these three stages? How well do they let go and let you enter and leave at your own will?

The bonding years are your main source of love, approval, and acceptance. The emotional bond that develops from birth on is an intricate web of feelings that gives you a sense of being bound together with loving parents. The texture of the family bond is colored by family experiences: whether you were originally wanted, whether you were loved or disliked, whether one of your parents was absent or withdrawn, whether your parent's marriage was a success or failure, and the general atmosphere in your family.

When you are small your parents play the part of protector and socializer. This is how you learn the rules of life and how to function with your family and in school with friends. Your mother or father controls your sense of well-being with love and acceptance. As you grow up you learn to cooperate with your family and at school. Your parents show anger and displeasure when you disobey the family rules. Some children fear the loss of their parents' love if they get in trouble. Parents should be wary of conveying negative feelings in this manner.

As a teenager you must remove yourself from the family bond in order to become independent. Many times this upsets your parents because it disrupts family routines. For you to successfully complete the task of puberty, to become yourself, you must unravel your bond with your parents. You must learn to cope as a separate person with your own personality, attitudes, and opinions. This is not easy for parents, nor for you, but it can and must be done.

This debonding is stressful in itself. It is stressful because there is no assurance of your future bonding with others during this time of breaking emotional ties with your family. It can cause even the most self-confident person to become insecure and scared.

You can debond from your parents by changing your mode of dress, changing from normal, average clothes to flashy, loud styles. You can debond by changing your way of talking. You can go from being shy and quiet to loud and obnoxious. Another way of debonding is by adopting different attitudes. Perhaps when you were younger you believed in going to church, or in joining groups at school. Now you have become a loner, with no special set of friends. Debonding is necessary. Children who cling to their parents, fearful of self-determination to do things on their own, remain childish throughout life. It takes guts to become your own person, but it is well worth doing. Go ahead. Try some things you have wanted to do. Believe in some things you want to believe in even if they are different from your family's beliefs.

A mutual rebonding occurs when a young adult leaves home as a separate person for the first time. Sometimes it does not happen until long afterward. Maybe there has been a rift between the young person and the parents. When they meet again after some time has elapsed, they look at things differently and can come together again as a family. It's a happy day when family members realize that they can still love someone who has a different way of thinking.

Important aspects of debonding from your parents are the following: (1) pulling away from your parents; (2) handling conflicting emotions; (3) working on your unfinished personality; (4) living with your peer loyalties; (5) dealing with questions and answers on love and sexuality; (6) respecting your intellectual growth; and (7) maintaining your physical well-being. Let's briefly discuss the seven debonding issues.

## PULLING AWAY FROM YOUR PARENTS

Both the female and male sexes begin their quest for independence by first debonding from their mother. The boy is usually first in seeking to define his masculinity, since it is more urgent. The girl moves from her mother more slowly, seeking assurance from her father. Young adults who experience debonding with their mother's acceptance become friendlier in high school. Other mothers use guilt to manipulate their children into spending time with them. Debonding can also occur in parents when they realize that they are being manipulative with their children by using guilt.

## CONFLICTING EMOTIONS

Who said being young was all fun and games? Young people are beset with conflicting emotions that cause wild mood swings. These contradictions in behavior can happen within an hour or a day. You can experience sheer exhilaration and utter despair all in one twenty-four-hour period. You will experience ups and downs in dealing with your parents, in trying to disconnect. Many rebellious acts are only ways of breaking ties with your family.

## UNFINISHED PERSONALITIES

As a young person your personality has not yet been totally defined. Believe it or not, you are still coming into yourself. Self-esteem begins in childhood, grows during the teenage years, and fluctuates widely during the adolescent process. You should have many areas from which to draw good feelings of worth. If you don't have a model's figure, use your intelligence. If you are not good in sports, try the field of music. If you are not very attractive, work on a sense of humor. Nobody can be everything, but everyone can be kind, considerate, and helpful to others. These traits will far outlast physical attributes. Beauty is nice but secondary to feelings of personal worth. People must have an inner warmth to earn friendship and love.

## PEER LOYALTIES

Banding together with friends who are also struggling with growing pains gives you a sense of belonging. Usually unwritten rules govern membership in a peer group. Some peer groups require excellent grades; others require participation in a certain sport or club. Still other peer groups require you to take drugs or drink or smoke. It is up to you to decide which group, if any, is the one to hang around with. The fear of being outcasts pressures members of high school cliques to adopt similar mannerisms of speech and dress. This conformity with a peer group satisfies your need for bonding while you are giving up your bonds with your parents. Sometimes this need to bond is so intense that young people bond with one special friend or a fantasy idol, one record, certain items of clothing. Peer loyalty is an authentic period of growth.

It's okay if you do not become involved with one peer group. It's okay if you are happy pursuing interests on your own. Many creative teenagers gain the needed approval by using their special talents. If you have a gift for creative writing, by all means use that gift. Perhaps you have a talent for gourmet cooking, or gardening, sewing, painting. Be proud of your talent and use it well. Not all people are blessed with talent, and someday it may become your livelihood.

## DEALING WITH LOVE AND SEXUALITY

Deeply interwoven with the emotional tasks of debonding are finding acceptance with peers, dealing with schoolwork, and learning to handle love and sexuality. The force of love is a powerful element beginning in childhood. Attachments are possible at any age. The upsurge of sexuality in teenagers and the feelings that accompany debonding from the family push them to displace family love onto other people such as friends and lovers. This love is authentic and intensive even if it is not permanent. Most teenagers take their love interests very seriously.

There is no such thing as unreal love. Love is the core feeling of life and is enriched first by family bonding and then by relationships outside the family. If your parents have a good relationship and love each other, they can empathize and sympathize with your romantic involvements. It is hoped that your parents can honestly discuss sex, birth control, and other important aspects of sexuality with you. If not, you need to find an older relative, a close neighbor, a teacher, or a school nurse with whom to talk. You can't always believe everything your friends tell you. Most often they are as confused as you are. Find an adult you can trust, and talk openly about love and sex.

## INTELLECTUAL GROWTH

The development of thought processes and perceptiveness escalates during your teenage years. You have the ability to imagine concepts and abstractions, pose hypothetical questions and answers, make logical deductions from scattered information, figure out solutions, create ideas, and think ahead to the future regarding possible consequences. This is an exciting time for intellectual growth.

Your possibilities seem limitless. You wonder about the meaning of life. Why are you here? What is your purpose? This surge of intellectual growth parallels your physical and sexual growth. All three of these cycles help you debond from your parents and leave childhood behind.

This is a wonderful time for your creative energies to come alive. They can be in music, art, writing. Go for it!

## PHYSICAL WELL-BEING

Your physical health is very important to your total well-being. Annual physical and dental checkups are necessary. A major problem for many teenagers is excessive weight. Nothing does more damage to self-esteem than being overweight. Fat teenagers are unhappy even if they hide their sadness from their families. If you have a weight problem, find help before it is too overwhelming to tackle. Some teenagers are lucky enough not to have to worry about what they eat, but at some point in our lives almost all of us have to watch our weight.

A disorder that mainly affects mid-adolescent girls is anorexia nervosa, a form of self-induced starvation. If untreated, this disorder can be fatal. A girl develops a delusional view of her body, seeing it as grossly overweight. She then starves herself into a skeletonlike figure. Food becomes digusting to her. Sometimes she gorges herself, then, feeling guilty for having given in to her appetite, throws up the food.

Anorexia nervosa requires immediate psychiatric care. The underlying motivation for self-induced starvation is usually an unconscious fear of growing into womanhood. Recent studies have shown that many girls with this disease also have severe problems with their father.

How is your relationship with your parents? Read Gena's story. What would you tell her to do to get along with her parents?

My name is Gena and I'm sixteen, but I feel a lot older. I feel as if I'm twenty or thirty the way my parents treat me. You see, I'm an only child. Some of my friends think that's the greatest thing in the world, but it isn't. Okay, so I get a lot of neat stuff, more than my friends who have sisters and brothers. But who can I share my things with? What's the fun of having anything if there is nobody to share it with?

My mom doesn't work, but she might as well. I

never see her. She's always doing things for other people and neglecting her own daughter. My father has this high-paying job. Big deal. Just because he makes a lot of money he thinks he can buy me love and attention. But I don't want material things. I want him. I want my father to treat me like a real, live person.

All my father thinks about is his job and how he can keep his job and do better at his job. He goes to work early and comes home late. If I'm lucky I may talk to him three times a week. If he happens to be at home, he is on the phone or listening to Mom and her complaints.

My mother is spoiled rotten by my dad. She doesn't know how good she has it. I look around at my friends' mothers and watch them work day in and day out. They work, come home, and eat and sleep. They never have time to really enjoy life as Mom does.

All Mom thinks about is herself. How she looks, how she feels. Every now and then she concerns herself with Dad, but not often. I ask her to go shopping with me for school clothes. No, she doesn't have time. Maybe next Saturday, but each Saturday becomes next Saturday.

Mom is in all of these garden clubs and do-goody clubs. She will go out of her way to visit some woman in the hospital, but does she ever have time for me? Did she come to my cheerleading tryouts? Did she ever talk to my algebra teacher when I was failing? She got me a tutor, but she never went to the school.

One time when I had a bad case of flu I had to stay home from school for a week. I loved it! Mom actually talked to me. We got to know each other as people. I almost hated getting well and going back to school.

Every now and then Dad likes to have these heart-to-heart talks with me. Usually it's when somebody dies and he feels guilty that he never has time for me. He asks me dumb stuff like what my goals are. I don't care about goals. I have a lifetime for that. But I do care about him knowing that I love him.

How come my parents never tell me they love me? Oh sure, I know they love me. I have my own room. I have beautiful clothes, anything I want. Except them. How can I have so much but so little?

My friend Sara is poor. I mean, her father ran out on her mother and her years ago. But Sara is happy. All she has is her mother, but boy, are they happy! When I go over there Sara and her mother always have plans to do something fun. They don't have a lot of money, but they have a lot of fun.

I just feel lonely. And I feel guilty. How can I complain about my parents when they give me everything I could ever want? They even have my college planned for and paid for. Now that's smart parents. But I want loving parents.

I've thought of doing something really stupid just to get their attention. You know, like running away from home. Or getting married. Maybe even getting pregnant! Maybe making straight F's on my report card. Maybe drugs.

I wonder if my parents really wanted me in the first place. I mean, they have all this money and I keep them from traveling and partying. What if I was a mistake? Were they so disappointed in me that they never wanted other children? Would they miss me if I died?

Gena's story is true. Gena has everything the world says

is important. But she does not have the one thing the world forgets: love. Gena knows she is loved, but she wants her parents to tell her so.

Gena is in counseling now with her parents. It is hard work, but they are making steady progress. If you too have special problems with your parental relationship, you can get help from one of the following people or places: your local family planning center, the YMCA or YWCA, your clergyperson, your school counselor or nurse, or a teacher you trust.

CHAPTER ◇ 2

# Just Between You and Your Siblings

The longest relationship you will ever have is the one with your siblings. Friends come and friends go. Family members pass on. You may even suffer the loss of one or both of your parents. Usually, though, when you look around in your life you will find a brother or a sister. In good times and bad times, brothers and sisters are there whether you want them to be or not.

But what is your relationship with your brother and sister? Are you close? Do you talk often? Growing up, you share unique experiences with your sibling. Treasure these experiences, because no one really knows you as your sibling does.

How may siblings do you have? Do you consider siblings to be a blessing or a curse in life? It depends on your individual family. In families where the parents practice fairness among the children, you may feel close to your sister. In other families where it is obvious to everyone who the favorite child is, you may not feel close to your brother, especially if you were not the favorite.

Birth order plays a major role in sibling relationships. Recent studies indicate that the first child is often the quietest and most dependable. More responsibility is placed on the first child. Firstborn children have a hard road to travel. Their parents were new at parenting, which often meant that they were strict and expected a lot. Parents are more nervous with their firstborn than any of the other children. Firstborn children are usually more successful in life because of their disciplined upbringing.

Second-born children are entirely different. For one thing, their parents have some experience in raising a child, which makes them more relaxed. Also, the second-born has an older sibling to model after.

Second-born children are very creative. Because their parents have been more at ease with them, they know no limits to their imagination. Determination to be what they want when they want is the hallmark of second-borns. These kids are happy-go-lucky. You will never find them with a stomach ulcer like the firstborn. Second-born children don't give a flip what anyone thinks.

Third-born children have the hardest shoes to fill. By the time they come along the parents are older. They know more about handling children, but they are too tired to always enforce the family rules. Third-born children are often the babies of the family. They get their way more often, but life is harder for them for that reason. The world doesn't care what order you were born in. Your family does.

Four major problems among you and your siblings are: (1) sibling rivalry; (2) expectations; (3) comparisons; and (4) acceptance. Let's discuss them and possible answers.

## SIBLING RIVALRY

What exactly is sibling rivalry? Rivalry is defined in the dictionary as trying to get the same thing as another; to do something better than another; to be equal to or as good as another. Sisters and brothers compete with each other constantly, whether they admit it or not. Who can get the best grades? Who can get the best-looking boyfriend? Who can get married first? Who makes the most money? This competition goes on throughout their lives. Who has the most expensive house? Who has the brightest children?

How can this be stopped? Sadly, sibling rivalry is taught in childhood by the parents. "Can you make as good grades as your brother?" Tommy's mother asks him on the first day of school. "I wonder who is going to have the most boyfriends?" Cindy's father asks as he looks at both of his daughters. This is indeed unfortunate. The world is hard enough; why compete within our own family? Not every child is going to make straight As. Not every child is going to be stunningly attractive. Why can't parents take each child as an individual? Why can't siblings take each other for the best, without hard feelings? We all have special talents. We all have faults. But in our family we need to love each other as ourselves. If you feel jealousy in your heart toward your sibling, go and talk with him or her. Don't carry unhappy thoughts about a person who should be one of your best friends in life. To have a sister or brother is special; enjoy it.

## EXPECTATIONS

What do you expect of your siblings? What do they expect of you? Do you expect undying loyalty? Do you expect them always to be there for you? Do you expect them to put you ahead of their family? Sit down and talk with your sibling about each other's expectations. You may be surprised. You may be shocked. But do it. Find out what your sibling expects of you.

Expectations come from each family. Many families get together only on special occasions, holidays, birthdays. Siblings see each other only when they are supposed to. How sad to put other things ahead of seeing a person you grew up with. Life gets hectic as we grow older, but we should always make time for our brothers and sisters.

## COMPARISONS

My sister is prettier than I. My brother is smarter than I. My sister gets to stay out later on dates than I do. My brother gets to go with Dad more. We all compare ourselves with others, especially with those closest to us. How come my hair is thin and my sister's is thick? How come my brother is so good in sports, and I can't even catch a ball? These are all normal questions. Many times it seems that our sibling got a better deal in life than we did. But look closer. Look beneath the surface. Your sister may be prettier than you, but you may be more creative than she. Your brother may be great in sports, but doesn't he always come to you for help with homework? We all have our weak points and our strong points. Be proud of your strong points and work on your weak ones.

Why compare yourself to someone who has the same parents as you, someone who shares your hard times and celebrates your good times? Your sibling is a part of yourself. Instead of comparing yourself with your sibling, why not help each other with weak points? Why not find something you enjoy doing together. Life is too short to compare yourself with your own flesh and blood.

## ACCEPTANCE

At some point in your life you will come to accept your siblings, come to accept them for themselves. With their faults and their good points. With their dazzling beauty and your average looks. With their superior intelligence and your average mind. With your large house and their cottage. With your good health and their awful disease.

Acceptance comes at odd moments. Sometimes it comes during an unexpected tragedy. It may come when one of you has a close brush with death or a severe illness. Perhaps acceptance will come during a happy time, a wedding, a celebration.

Acceptance of your sibling does not always come easily. It may take years to work through hurtful memories of a boyfriend lost to your sister or a game lost to your brother. Maybe you were the family favorite and your sisters and brothers resent you. Maybe you were the last person to see your parents alive. Maybe you were the one who could do no wrong.

Achieving anything of value takes time, work, and patience. Work and talk through any sensitive subject you may have with your siblings. Don't let anything come between you. As time goes on, you will realize how lucky you are to have them. Not everyone is so lucky.

Let's consider the story of Susan and her sister Amy. Listen to both sides. What would you do?

## SUSAN

My name is Susan and I'm fourteen. And I'm sick to death of hearing about my sister Amy. Amy this and Amy that. Amy is a cheerleader. Amy is on the honor roll. Amy has four boyfriends. Amy is a size six.

Amy never forgets Grandmother's birthday. Amy is so pretty she can become a model. Amy is so smart she can become a doctor. I mean, if you hang around my family at all you will hear the wonderful story of perfect Amy. The only problem is that I have to live with her.

And then there is me. Ugly, fat, dumb me. Maybe I'm not so ugly, fat, and dumb. But when you compare me to Amy I'm all of the above. It's not that I hate myself so much, it's that everyone adores Amy so much.

The worst part of it is that Amy is actually nice to me. Beautiful, perfect Amy helping miserable me. And she's nice about it too. You never hear her complaining when she has to turn down dates with senior guys to help me with algebra. I bet Amy could do algebra when she was born. I have already failed algebra once.

Everything comes easy to Amy. I have to struggle and fight for everything I get. She even cooks. On top of being head cheerleader, Amy helps Mom in the kitchen. She helps Dad with the yard. And she still makes good grades and has friends.

I have one friend, Angela. But Amy says Angela just comes over to flirt with Rod, our brother. My best friend, Sue, moved to Wyoming last summer. I felt so lonely. Amy had gone to cheerleading camp.

Amy is always trying to help me with my makeup and hair. But even with makeup I don't look as pretty as she does. She once even tried to fix me up on a blind date with her last boyfriend's brother. What a joke! Nobody told us he was twenty-five.

One time when Amy was sick, it was really strange. I went to school and everyone asked me about her.

One time when I was sick and Mom went to get my home work, the teacher didn't even know I was absent. That made me feel good!

I feel guilty talking about Amy like this. She's been a super sister to me despite the hateful things I've done to her. Like the time I put a dead mouse in her purse and she passed out cold in French class. Ha. She didn't talk to me for three days. Or the time I lied to one of her teachers about her skipping school. Boy, did I get in trouble for that one!

Amy never tries to get even with me. I keep expecting something dreadful to happen someday, but nothing ever does. Is Amy perfect, everyone asks me? No. She never picks up her dirty clothes on the floor. She never unplugs the blow dryer in the bathroom. She squeezes the top of the toothpaste instead of the bottom. She eats too much junk food but never gains an ounce. I gain by just looking at food!

I want to get over my intense jealousy of Amy, but I don't know where to turn.

## AMY

My name is Amy and I'm sixteen. I have a little sister, Susan, who is a pistol. She has this horrible self-image, and it's getting worse. I get a lot of attention and that drives Susan wild with envy. I keep telling her to get out and make some of her own attention, but she just nods her head and switches the TV to another channel. Susan wants a lot of things, but she doesn't want to work for them.

She weighs about twenty pounds over her ideal weight. Does she ever try to lose it? No. She eats constantly. I tell her that three chocolate bars before bed go straight to her hips. I try to help her with her makeup and hair, but she argues over everything I try.

Susan is smart, but she doesn't study. She would rather sit and talk on the phone about some rock group. Susan is pretty in her own way, but she refuses to experiment with any new hair style or lipstick. She would rather sleep late in the morning than get up early and curl her hair.

She could be on the pep squad, but she never made practice so they kicked her out. She doesn't have many friends because she is always graphing about something. She hurts Mom's feelings when she forgets her birthday. Susan thinks only about herself, nobody else.

She thinks I have it so much easier than she. Well, she's wrong. I work very hard for everything I get. Susan doesn't remember the times I got up early in the summer to practice for cheerleader. She forgets about the times I study until midnight to keep myself on the honor roll. She forgets that I constantly watch my diet and that I have given up my favorite foods such as pizza and chocolate to stay a size six. She forgets that I work hard to keep a boyfriend. You have to work at a relationship; you don't just wish it. I try to help Susan with her homework. Sometimes she will let me and other times she won't. It depends on her mood at the moment. When she is desperate enough, she will ask me for help. If she can get help from somebody else, she will.

I feel sorry for Susan most of the time, and the rest of the time I want to kill her. She feels so sorry for herself when there are so many people worse off than she is. For example, take Kelly Sims. She is sixteen, has cancer, and her parents are getting a divorce. But does that stop Kelly? No way. Kelly is a cheerleader. Kelly is in the band. Kelly makes the honor roll. Maybe it is because she knows she can't waste time.

Susan takes everything for granted as if we will always be here. She's wrong. Last week Wendy Wilson was killed in a car wreck after school. It really shook Susan up, because Wendy often drove Susan home. What if Susan had been with Wendy that afternoon?

Another friend of ours, Sheila Parker, is in the hospital with muscular dystrophy. I think I'll take Susan with me next time I visit Sheila. I'll see if she has a different attitude after she sees Sheila laid up in that bed all day. Sheila of all people—Sheila who was head majorette, Sheila who was first-chair flute in the concert band.

What do you do with a sister like Susan? Some people tell me to accept her the way she is. I want to, but I hate to see her miserable every single day of her life. And her being unhappy affects me, and Mom and Dad too. She bites our heads off first thing in the morning and the last thing before bed. I hate to be around her for any length of time.

What can I do for my sister?

Susan and Amy are suffering from sibling rivalry. It's the classic story: one sister beautiful, popular, and well adjusted; one sister average, lonely, and miserable.

Things got worse between the sisters. Their parents decided that they all needed to go to a family counselor. After six weeks of group therapy, this is what the counselor commented:

Susan and Amy needed help. Underneath all their backbiting, all their bitterness, and their hate, I sensed a bond of real love. Thanks to caring, sensitive parents, Susan and Amy came to me in time to help them quite a bit.

Susan and Amy are both frustrated with growing up. For one thing, it is harder than they expected. They have been reading far too many romance novels and seeing too many silly movies. Life is hard, and they want it to be easy. They both want life to be fair, and it just isn't.

It is true that Amy has a striking appearance and Susan a rather plain one. But Susan is just as much loved in her family as Amy is. The problem is that Susan doesn't accept herself. Susan has to learn to accept herself and love herself before she can accept or love anyone else.

To like anyone else, you have to like yourself first. Susan is too hard on herself. So she isn't perfect; who is? Most people learn to cover their faults and to flaunt their strong points. Amy is an excellent example of this.

Susan needs to have something that she can excel in, something to take her mind off herself. As Amy suggested, Susan could do volunteer work at the hospital or a rest home. Susan needs to get her mind off of Susan. There is a whole big world out there, and she needs to lose herself in it.

Amy is fairly well adjusted and happy with herself for her age. She has a lot of self-confidence and personality. Life will be easy for Amy. Life will be hard for Susan, but she can make it easier by helping herself.

The outlook is good for these sisters. Their sibling

relationship is vital because from it they will form their other relationships.

The sisters' parents came in for several sessions. They admitted that it is easier to love Amy because she has fewer problems. Susan needs any positive reinforcement she can get. I talked with some of her teachers, and they are aware of her problems. These two sisters and their family are going to make it.

If you need someone to talk to, these people can help: A family counselor, an adolescent counselor, or a mental health counselor; a psychologist or psychotherapist.

# CHAPTER 3

# Surviving a Death
# in the Family

**N**othing in this world can ever prepare you for a death in your immediate family. Nothing. It is a unique experience, a sorrow known only to the person grieving. You will never be the same person again. Never will you look at life in the same way again. Someone has said that grief never puts us back where we were when we met it. Emerging from deep sorrow is like coming in out of a hailstorm: it hurts us, but we dry ourselves off and go on with life.

Life is hard, and losing someone we love, a close family member, is one of the hardest things we endure. We don't know why this special person is taken from us, but we go on because we know it is our only choice. Life is for the living. You can always remember this person in special ways, but never must you give in to your grief totally and give up on life.

How long does it take to get over losing a family member? Is there a process we go through? What can we do to get through those first hard hours and days? Whom do we talk to? Does anyone really care about our intense feelings? Will I ever get over this terrible, aching sadness? What if I never feel happy again?

There is no timetable to grief. It depends on the person grieving and the person lost. Some people seem to bounce back into the mainstream of life. Others seem to face a long winding road that never ends. Just remember that others have traveled this lonely road and have emerged. You can too.

Grieving is a definite process. When you lose a loved one your first reaction is shock. No, this can't be true. This cannot be happening to my family. Denial follows. No, I will not accept this tragedy in my family. It will go away, and things will be the same as they were. This is just a bad dream. Anger follows denial. This is not fair! It is not fair that my wonderful father has to die of cancer when there are so many awful people in the world still alive! Believe it or not, anger is the stage that can help you cope better than the others can. After anger, guilt follows. Did I do enough for this person? Was I kind enough? What about the time we had that argument? What about the time I lied? Depression follows guilt. I don't care anymore about life. I don't care what happens to me. Finally acceptance comes. Blessed acceptance comes, for we could not continue carrying this hugh load of emotional baggage.

The most difficult task any young person can undertake is trying to make sense out of the death of a parent. The great stabilizer of our life is gone. So many questions are unanswered. So many feelings are ignored. Young people don't need to hear platitudes after they have encountered one of the biggest shocks of their lives. You deserve the same respect for your pain as any adult deserves and expects. You are hurting. You need answers. Mainly you need someone to talk to. Hour after hour. Day after day. Find that special friend to help you put your shattered heart back together. No, your heart will never fit in that perfect puzzle again, but you can make a new puzzle. You can become a newer, stronger person. Show the world that although your heart may be broken, you're not broken.

Whom do you talk to after this life-altering experience? Who cares? Who has the time to sit and hold your hand and promise you that the sun will still rise every morning?

Talk to your remaining parent. He or she is suffering too. What about your siblings? What about relatives? Talk to a caring teacher at school, or the school counselor. Talk to your clergyperson or a friend at church or temple. It is vital that you do find someone to talk to. Keeping your feelings bottled up does your body physical harm. The feelings are going to come out in one way or another. Let them come out the natural way. It's okay to talk about your parent's death. It's no sin to wonder why, ask why, cry out loud why? It's normal and healthy to ask why.

During the first few weeks and months after your loss, your body is under tremendous stress, physically and emotionally. In these times it's hard to remember to take extra care of yourself. Your body defenses are down, and it is easy to become ill. Get plenty of rest. Try to eat three balanced meals a day though you may not be hungry. If you don't feel like going to school, don't. One week off should be sufficient for you to get hold of yourself. Remember, you and your body have undergone a terrible strain. After losing a parent you need time to heal. Healing and acceptance don't come overnight. Don't expect it, and don't be hard on yourself.

In this stressful time you may encounter some peculiar problems. You may have trouble concentrating at school. You may have trouble sleeping or eating. Maybe you are experiencing nightmares and sweating. You may lose weight or gain weight. You may feel achy all over and just not your usual self. That is normal. These symptoms will pass in time.

A good way to begin to cope after a dreadful loss is to take up that hobby you have always wanted to do. Take dancing lessons. Take painting lessons, or music, or a creative writing course. Do anything that will help take your mind off your loss. Do some volunteer work at the hospital or a rest homes. Get out and talk to other people. You will be surprised at how good it will feel to take your mind off yourself, even if for a day. Who knows? That hobby might someday turn your entire life around.

Believe it or not, your life will go on without your parent. Time is the great healer, and one day you will find yourself laughing and going on with your life. Not in the same way, but nevertheless going on. You will look at things in a different way. Sorrow teaches many lessons along the way, and you will be much the wiser person.

Take heart. Someday you will be comforting friends who have lost a parent, and you will say that your life has gone on and theirs will too.

"Forgotten grievers" is a term applied to children who experience the loss of a sister or brother. Perhaps they could also be called the lonely mourners. Whom do you turn to when you have lost a sister or brother? Your parents? No. They are overwhelmed by their own devastating pain. You are lost in your own private sea of pain. People come to talk with your parents in the living room while you mourn your loss alone in your bedroom. It is a frustrating and heartbreaking situation. Somehow people think there is nothing to losing a brother or sister. How wrong. Losing a sibling can mean everything, losing your best and only friend, losing some of your childhood.

Added to the forgotton grievers' burden of loneliness and grief is the possibility that they had a love-hate relationship with the one who has died? The love is natural, but competitive human nature interferes.

After a death, whether we are young children or adults, instead of remembering all the good times we shared, we remember the times we shouted angrily or slapped and punched, creating tremendous guilt.

The range of problems and needs that the surviving sibling encounters is almost limitless. You may ask: "Will this soon happen to me?" "Are my parents going to die next?" "It should have been me, why wasn't it?" "My sister was my parents' favorite, and they don't care about me." "God must be punishing me for being mean to my brother." The saddest comment of all—"I'm all alone now. I've lost my parents too, because they talk about nothing but the one has died."

In the United States alone over 400,000 children under the age of twenty-five die each year from catastrophic illness, infant diseases, suicide, murder, and accidents. Large numbers of these children are survived by siblings numbering in the millions. Millions of surviving siblings who are yearning to be understood. These millions become tens of millions with each year also bringing the death of adult children over twenty-five who die before their parents. The emotions experienced by siblings after the death of a sister or brother are rooted in early childhood relationships.

Several problems are encountered by the remaining sibling. Parents tend to overprotect the survivor, afraid to allow normal activities. Surviving children are often haunted by the fear of something untoward happening to their parents. Another problem is parents who remind survivors of the dead child at family events, graduations, weddings, birthdays. Sometimes a surviving child wants to hold onto something that belonged to the dead sibling, a piece of jewelry, a scarf, a shirt. Parents often resent seeing their living child wearing an object that was worn by the dead sibling.

How do you cope with holidays and anniversaries? Many surviving sisters and brothers do well for months and then suddenly become depressed at approaching holidays or the anniversary of a sibling's death. These reactions are normal. Parents need to remember that they still have a child alive, and life goes on. In talking about how siblings heal after the loss of a brother or sister, communication and having someone to share thoughts with are all-important.

Let's talk to one survivor who lost a sister and see how she handled it.

Heather Collins was a surviving sister who was tired of hearing, "I know how you feel." "It makes me so mad when people say that, because unless they lost a brother or sister they don't know how I feel. My parents had each other to comfort, but my sister Annie was part of me, my closest friend, and I have no one to comfort me, no one who knows how I really feel."

"After the funeral I did not want to see anyone. I knew it upset my parents, but I told them to tell everyone to just leave me alone. There was one woman, though, for whom I baby-sat. Her name was Lisa. A week before Annie died, her sister had died in a car accident. So when Lisa came to see me in my bedroom and said, 'Heather, I know how you feel,' I knew she really did know."

Heather was very bitter about the help she and her sister had sought but failed to receive from psychologists. The psychologists kept Heather from seeing her sister the last two weeks of her life. Instead Heather received counseling from therapists, social workers, and ministers.

Each person is unique and expresses pain differently. Outwardly some surviving brothers and sisters may appear to have coped with grief successfully, but inwardly they continue to suffer. But, like parents, siblings learn to control their grief in that they don't consciously think of it every minute. Siblings and parents can live a good and complete life, but they can't expect to be the way they were before. It is normal to remember the dead, but that remembering does not preclude getting on with life. The important thing is not that our brothers or sisters died, but that they lived.

To help you with your loss, here is a list of organizations designed just for that. It's okay to reach out for help; someday someone may be reaching out for your help.

Candlelighters and the Candlelighter Foundation Candlelighters is an international organization of people who have lost children to cancer. Some groups have youth auxiliaries for teenage cancer patients and for teenage siblings of cancer victims. The groups provide counseling for the family. Candlelighters has more that 165 chapters. For more information write or call:
The Candlelighters Foundation
1901 Pennsylvania Avenue NW
Washington DC 20006
(202) 659-5136

Centers for Attitudinal Research
This organization was developed by a child psychiatrist for children with life-threatening illnesses. It directs its attention to children from six to sixteen and offers a sharing, loving, supportive program with the use of art and music. Siblings of children who have

died need to share their fears. In the siblings' group, common fears about anger and guilt feelings about sick or dying brothers and sisters are discussed in a supportive atmosphere. For more information write or call:

The Center for Attitudinal Healing
19 Main Street
Tiburon, Ca 94920
(415) 435-5022

Compassionate Friends, Inc.
This voluntary self-help organization offers understanding and friendship to bereaved parents and surviving siblings. Its main goal is to assist families in the positive resolution of their grief after the death of a child and to promote their physical and emotional health. The group charges no dues and has no religious affiliation. Founded in England, it now has 525 chapters in the United States as well as chapters in England, Australia, South Africa, The Netherlands, Canada, Israel, and Switzerland. It also publishes pamphlets as guides in understanding for teachers, doctors, and nurses. For more information, write or call:

Compassionate Friends, Inc.
P.O. Box 3696
Oak Brook, IL 60522-3696
(312) 990-0010

Living Is for Today (LIFT)
An open-ended self-help support goup, LIFT is sponsored by Bereavement Services & Community Education, a division of Humphrey Funeral Home. It hosts weekly meetings open to the community and offers grieving siblings support, encouragement, and

a common language. Each group is facilitated by a professionally trained person. There are no attendance or financial requirements. For more information write or call:
Diana McKendree, Director
Bereavement Services & Community Education
1403 Bayview Avenue
Toronto, Ontario, Canada M4G 3A8
(416) 485-6415

MADD (Mothers Against Drunk Drivers)
This group was founded by Candy Lightner after her thirteen-year-old daughter was killed by a repeat-offender drunk driver. It includes not only fathers, sons, daughters, and siblings but also concerned citizens. The national aims are to enforce legislation to take drunk drivers off the road; to provide victim support; and to further public awareness. For more information, write or call:
Norma Phillips, President
Mothers Against Drunk Drivers
669 Airport Freeway, Suite 310
Hurst, TX 76053
(817) 268-MADD

Parents of Murdered Children, Inc.
This self-help group believes that a person who has recovered from a loss can be more helpful than a professional using only theoretical knowledge. Often siblings attend meetings, and some chapters have sibling groups. Families of a homicide death have to bear an additional burden to grief—that of intrusion into their intense grief. The news media focus on the victim and the family. Police, lawyers, and others may require information, testimony. If a murder suspect is

apprehended, further pain ensues: hearings, trials, postponements, sentences pronounced, all taking their toll on the family. For more information, write or call:

Parents of Murdered Children, Inc.
1739 Bella Vista
Cincinnati, OH 45237
(513) 242-8025

Rothman-Cole Center for Sibling Loss
The center provides individual and family counseling, focusing solely on sibling bereavement. For more information write or call:

Rothman-Cole Center for Sibling Loss
1456 West Montrose Avenue
Chicago, IL 60613
(312) 769-0185

Survivors of Suicide
P.O. Box 1393
Dayton, OH 45406

TIGERS (Teens in Grief: educate, rebuild, support)
This is a grief support group for teenage surviving siblings. Write to:

Fr. Mike DiMaio, Grief Facilitator
521 Garden Court
Quincy, IL 62301
or
Ingrid Prunkl, Therapist
2811 Kingsridge
Quincy, IL 62301

# CHAPTER 4

# Dealing With Serious Illness in the Family

**V**ery few people get through life without some personal or family crisis. Most crises are self-limiting or resolve themselves in time, but others may require professional help. It is practically certain that you or a member of your family will have occasion to use the services of one of a variety of health professionals.

This chapter discusses five major illnesess that afflict a quarter of a million Americans: (1) mental illness; (2) AIDS; (3) alcoholism; (4) cancer; and (5) handicaps. These problems have no perfect solutions, but the illnesses can be handled in a way that is conducive to positive living. Above all, a positive and hopeful attitude is vital.

## MENTAL ILLNESS

Mental illness is such a slippery term that we find ourselves substituting others for it—mentally disturbed, severely disturbed, troubled, disordered, distressed. They turn out to be just as slippery. Medical professionals use terms such as neurotic, psychotic, paranoid, schizoid, and schizophrenic. In the old days people were just called crazy.

The most common form of mental illness is neurosis. Neurosis may be viewed as expressions of conflict—conflict between impulse and reality, between one impulse and another, between desires and duties that are irreconcilable. Conflict is normal; we all express it in our daily lives. Conflict may be conscious or unconscious.

Most of us accept conflicts as part of life. They may cause temporary upsets, but they pass and we go on. But some upsets are not temporary, and some responses are out of proportion to the actual situation. People who have difficulty adapting to conflicts, who overract to their situation, may be called neurotic.

A person who fails to adapt to these stresses may express his maladaptation in various ways—through depression, anxiety, sleeping or eating disorders, or excessive drinking. Neurotics repeat the the same behavior patterns over and over.

Other mental illnesses include phobias (strong and unreasonable fears) and psychomatic disorders. Emotional factors contribute heavily to illnesses such as ulcers, asthma, obesity, high blood pressure. Our bodies and minds are so linked that doctors estimate that more than half the ailments they treat have a psychological component. The last two major mental illnesses are schizophrenia and depression. Schizophrenics have a distorted, fragmented view of reality. The diagnosis of depression is a matter of degree. The depressed person feels tired, hopeless, powerless. Severe depression can be treated with drugs.

Mental illness is America's primary public health problem. It costs us $21 billion yearly and strikes 10 percent of the population.

## AIDS

Between 1981 and 1986 some 12,000 people died of the disease AIDS. What is this deadly disease? It is the virus that causes acquired immunodeficiency syndrome, the worst public health disaster ever. AIDS is disturbing because it kills and because there is no vaccine for it and no cure. Like leprosy and the Black Death in the Dark Ages, AIDS seems to work in mysterious ways. It is transmitted by sexual contact, but little else is known about it.

Evidence from Africa and most recent statistics from the United States report that AIDS is not a "gay plague" and that the virus is in fact indifferent to its victim's sexual orientation. More and more heterosexuals are contracting the disease, at a time when its rate of increase is slowing among homosexual males.

The AIDS virus does not attack only the immune system; it lives and replicates in the brain and the cerebrospinal fluid. It then is a nightmare process of brain atrophy. The effects include personality changes, epileptic fits, progressive memory loss, and complete neural failure. The average cost of medical care for one AIDS patient in the United States is $100,000.

How do you live with a family member who has AIDS? Give and help find for that person a will to live. Don't forget the power of human contact and love. We all need to be loved and touched. Give your loved one a purpose in life. What is the most important thing to tell an AIDS patient and the family? To love and support each other. That's the most important gift we have. No disease is more isolating, more lonely then AIDS. A parent's love is the most important factor in comforting the AIDS victim.

## ALCOHOLISM

Alcoholism is known as the "family disease" because each member of the alcoholic's family is affected as well. Children of alcoholics grow up in dysfunctional families, full of fear, anger, and denial, and they suffer emotional or physical abuse as well. When these children grow up and have families of their own, they bring their past into their relationships with their spouse, friends, and employers.

What is an alcoholic? Seven million kids under the age of twenty live with an alcoholic parent. Alcoholics tend to display some or all or these characteristics: He or she lies about how much he has had to drink; always has a good reason to drink; argues when drunk; can't stop drinking until he is drunk; blames others for the drinking; and denies things done while drinking.

Characteristics commonly found in alcoholic families are the following:

- It's not okay to talk about problems.
- Feelings should not be expressed openly.
- Communication is often indirect.
- Expectations are unrealistic.
- Don't be selfish; that gets turned around to mean take care of others and not yourself.
- Do as I say, not as I do.
- It's not okay to play. Life is serious, difficult and painful, not a joyful world in which kids can be spontaneous.

For the families of alchoholics, particularly the children, alcoholism can twist parenting into a form of child abuse. Even if you grow up with no physical abuse, just having a drinker around the house warps family relationships. You and your problem drinker need to get help.

## CANCER

Cancer is a major illness, but not necessarily fatal. Nearly two million Americans are considered cured of cancer five years or more after their initial diagnosis. One in three people with cancer is cured. For some froms of the disease, nine out of ten people diagnosed can be considered cured. Many others will live a long time before dying of the disease. Yet the diagnosis of cancer is the most dreaded of any medicaal problem. The first question is how long will I live? No one really knows.

There is hope for every patient. Some patients are cured by surgery, chemotherapy, or radiotherapy. Some patients are never cured, but their disease it controlled so that they can live for many years.

Treatments are not easy. In some cases they cause hair loss, nausea, or the loss of a limb or breast. These losses can be worse than the actual disease.

Just what is cancer? Cancer is a group of diseases in which there is irregular growth of abnormal cells. Normal cells grow in an orderly, controlled pattern; as they wear out and die, new ones are produced. Abnormal cells grow in an uncontrolled pattern; they never stop reproducing themselves.

The medical specialty that deals with cancer is oncology, and the specialist who treats it is an oncologist.

## HANDICAPS

If you have had a broken arm in a cast for several months, you remember how helpless you felt and how embarrassed you were that you needed help. Those who have had worse problems such as a broken back and were confined in a body cast for weeks recall what it is like to be immobile.

But those are only temporary handicaps. The people know that they will get better; their condition will improve, and they will be whole again.

That is not the case with handicapped people. Their condition is theirs for life. Either they adjust and go on with life, or they rebel, become bitter, and sour their lives. How well they adjust and overcome problems determines their success and happiness in life.

What does the word handicapped mean? As defined in the dictionary, a handicap is anything that holds a person back or gives him less of a chance than others have.

Examples of handicaps are cerebral palsy, muscular dystrophy, paralysis, mental retardation, speech handicap, and learning disorder, to name just a few.

How can you help loved ones live a full life with their handicap? Let them do what they can. Don't let them lean on you too much. Let them make their mistakes and learn from them. It's all a part of life.

How does your handicapped loved one feel about himself? The way he sees himself plays a big role in the way he adjusts to life. Handicapped people feel self-conscious. They need recognition. Find something special that the handicapped person can do well and praise him for it. So Johnny in his wheelchair can't play football, he has a wonderful singing voice. Praise Johnny for his voice. Encourage him to sing as much as possible. So Karen can't try out for cheerleader since her car accident, but she writes very well. Praise Karen every chance you get. Encourage her to polish her writing skills. Everyone is talented in one area or another, including the handicapped.

What happens when handicapped people do not like themselves? You must help them build a sense of personal worth, a feeling of security from within. Handicapped persons must have faith; they must have faith in themselves, faith in their parents, and faith in their doctors.

Help your handicapped loved one develop these important personality traits: self-acceptance, self-actualization; self-assertiveness; self-consistency; self-criticism; self-determination; self-realization; and self-regard.

We must all accept life for what it is. We are all vulnerable to pain and suffering. In human life fairness has nothing to do with illness, divorce, death, accidents, shattered dreams. The world cannot be what we want it to be.

Accept your life, whatever its handicaps, whatever its problems and heartaches. Accept your life and it will accept you.

Consider Sharon's story of heartache, disappointment, depression, and finally acceptance of her own tragic handicap.

If only I had listened to my dad that September night four years ago. But I didn't. I was sixteen and thought I knew it all. How wrong I was! And that one mistake almost cost me my life.

Steve Smith had called me that night as I was helping Mom clear the dinner table. Steve was cute, popular, and had a brand new sports car. I could not believe he actually called me first. But he did and said he wanted to give me ride in his new car. Mom looked at Dad, and Dad shook his head no right away without even thinking. I threw a small fit and said that I deserved to go out and have fun during the week. Dad said he wanted me to have fun, but not with Steve Smith. He said he knew Steve's parents, and they had no control over Steve. No, Dad did not want me going out with Steve. But I sneaked out my bedroom window and went anyway. The next time I saw my parents was in the hospital, changed forever.

Needless to say, Steve was showing off, driving his new car very fast. He also had been drinking. At first it was fun screaming down the streets, but then I got scared. Steve would not pull over and let me out. I was stuck in a speeding car with a drunk teenager.

I thought we were going to make it home, but just as Steve was rounding the corner to my block he lost control of the car. We went flying around the corner at such speed that I was literally thrown out.

The next thing I knew I was in the hospital with only one leg. They had to amputate my left leg because of the extensive injuries. I was lucky to be alive, but I didn't feel so at the time. I had just made head cheerleader the day before. Who ever heard of a one-legged cheerleader?

Steve was not even hurt seriously. He was so drunk that his body did not tense up at the moment of impact as mine did. It made me sick. The accident was his fault in the first place, and he goes unscratched. I'm left with a hideous deformity.

I will always love Dad even more because when he walked into my hospital room he could have said, "I told you so," but he didn't. I've accepted my handicap now. It's taken a few years, but life goes on. I'm in college now and dating a nice guy who doesn't drink.

## WHERE TO GET HELP

*For Mental Illness:*
The National Association for Mental Health

The National Association for Retarded Citizens
The Association for Children with Learning Disabilities

*For AIDS:* (Tapes and resources)
AIDS, A Positive Approach/Louise Hay
AIDS, Doors Opening/Louise Hay
AIDS Project
7362 Santa Monica
Los Angeles, CA 90046

*For Alcohism*
Alcoholics Anonymous
Box 459, Grand Central Station
New York, NY 10163

*For the Handicapped*
Department of Health and Human Services
Washington DC 20201

International Society for Rehabilitation of the Disabled
219 East 44th Street
New York, NY 10017

Americn Physical Therapy Association
1740 Broadway
New York, NY 10019

*For Cancer*
Cancer Information Services
1-800-4-CANCER

American Cancer Society
90 Park Avenue
New York, NY 10016

I CAN COPE
90 Park Avenue
New York, NY 10016

MAKE TODAY COUNT
P.O.Box 222
Osage Beach, MO 65065

United Cancer Council, Inc.
650 East Carmel Drive
Carmel, IN 46032

# CHAPTER 5

# When Someone in Your Family Is a Runaway

One million children run away each year. The National Center for Health Statistics reports that one youth in ten between the ages of twelve and seventeen had run away from home at some point in their lives. One thing they all have in common is that they're young and they hurt. Most have had a fight with a parent.

Peak runaway times coincide with the first warm week of spring, just after school has closed for the summer, or when school opens and parents start putting on the pressure to do well. Other times of running away are when report cards are passed out and after the Christmas holidays (when teenagers like adults fall victim to postholiday blues). Runaways today generally stick close to home. Automobile drivers' fear of being robbed makes it harder to thumb rides than it used to be. More kids from working-class and low-income homes are splitting, and they're less used to long-distance travel.

Most runaways are between fourteen and sixteen, but the age is dropping. A Metropolitan Washington Council on Government study on runaways youths in the Washington area reports that a growing number are in the eleven to thirteen age bracket.

More girls than boys run away. Boys don't show up at runaway shelters as girls are apt to do. Parents don't report boys missing as much as girls. Girls are more likely than boys to run away with friends or to team up with someone they meet on the road. Less use of drugs is found among runaways; most kids no longer consider smoking pot as "drug use." Most runaways stay away only one to three days. The longer a teenager is on the road, the greater the chances that he won't return home. The more often a youth runs away, the longer he is apt to stay. Sooner or later the chronic runaway remains gone forever.

The name of the game for runaways is survival. They have to eat, have somewhere to sleep, and have connections. They have to depend on the goodwill of friends and strangers whom they can't always trust. Runaways most often turn to friends. They use a friend's house as shelter. The friend's parents don't realize that the kid in their son's bedroom is running away from home, so they don't do anything.

Legally minors lack many of the rights that adults have. They can't work without permits, which parents or guardians must approve. In some school districts they can't enroll without parental or guardian sponsorship. In some states doctors will not treat a minor without a parent or a guardian present. If runaways are under eighteen they have trouble renting hotel and motel rooms even if they pay in advance; hotels don't want to be accused of harboring runaways. Most states require parental permission for a teenager to obtain a driver's license. For juvenile runaways, the aim is to keep from being picked up by the police. In nine states a runaway child comes within the jurisdiction of the juvenile court as a delinquent child, in fifteen others as a child in need of supervision.

Kids who run away find it harder to survive today than a few years ago. The economic situation makes people less generous, and the fear of crime makes people reluctant to help strangers, even young ones. Panhandling isn't as easy as it used to be, although girls do much better at it than boys. Free food programs have been dropped even in tolerant cities such as San Francisco. Mission beds have disappeared. Runaways become street-smart fast. They have to.

What makes kids run away from home? One of the leading reasons is abusive parents. Kids don't know how to get a positive response from their parents, but they do know how to get a negative response: They run away from home.

Next to sibling incest, father-daughter incest is the most common kind and the most common reason girls leave home. Incest is far more prevalent than is realized. Many girls run away because of a stepfather. He is aroused by the budding young woman and forces or persuades her to perform some sexual act. Eventually the girl is so overcome by shame or guilt feelings that she runs away.

Incest occurs in homes where the parents' relationship is poor both emotionally and sexually. They lack control over their impulses. Often the father drinks heavily and has a violent temper; many have affairs outside the home.

Another reason teens run away is divorce. The teenager lives with a single parent and siblings. The mother is harried, depressed, lonely, and has money problems. She can't cope with all the demands on her, so the oldest teenager is pressed into service as a mini-parent. The teenager resents all that responsibility and runs away. Sometimes children who live with a divorced parent run away to be with the other parent.

What are the characteristics of runaways? They are impulsive. They are easily distracted and act on impulse. They can't bear to delay gratification; they can't tolerate frustration. They may have an uncontrollable temper, be lonely and withdrawn, or cling desperately to peer groups. Runaways do not trust adults. They have low self-esteem.

What do runaway teens need most? Parents who give them lots of love and teach them self-respect and self-determination.

What if one of your parents runs away? What are the circumstances that drive men and women to disappear from their families? An accumulation of anger, resentment, disappointments, unmet expectations in relation to their spouse and possibly their children. Men may face a financial crisis, fail to get an expected raise or promotion, or lose a job. Others leave simply for a change in life or to better their status. An unhappy home life is an element in all runaways by adults.

Men may run away because of wives who are never happy, never satisfied. They point to wives who nag and complain, wives who have affairs, wives who have changed. "She's not the woman I married," is a common statement from runaway husbands. There are men who run away with other women and men who run away with other men. Some men in their middle years decide they are more "comfortable" with homosexual alliances and run away because they can't face wife and family.

Men run away during their "midlife crisis," a time when

a man takes stock of his life and finds it not to his liking. But they soon find that there's no perfect life and try to return home—where in many cases it is too late. A few men end up losing everything, as suicides, mental patients, or Skid Row bums.

Some men run away to escape alimony and child support payments. According to the Office of Child Support Enforcement, close to 3.3 million absent parents are associated with welfare families.

How do runaway men survive? Some take money from a joint bank account before departing. Others take off with the car and the family savings.

Most men run away impulsively with nothing but the clothes on their backs. All they know is that they can't take it anymore. Some leave for work after kissing their wife good-bye and never return home. Some leave notes, some don't. Some call, some don't.

What about women who run away? Women run away from situations that they view as intolerable.

In their late twenties or thirties or forties, they see themselves as victims of emotional neglect. Some want their husband to pay more attention to them. Some feel that their husband treats them like a child. Some feel they have grown beyond their husband intellectually. Many have for years begged their husband to change, and the husband has ignored their pleas. These wives cling to the hope that their running away will bring about those changes.

Battered wives leave their husbands because the threat is always present in their lives. Some have been brutalized for years and have finally had enough. Others go when their children are threatened.

One woman took a year to save five hundred dollars before leaving. Wives more often than husbands leave a note behind. Women are more careful of running away than men. Yet like men, they realize all too soon that there is no perfect mate or life.

Where do they go? For the runaway who needs to watch every dime, the YWCA is the only hope. Many large cities have shelters for battered women. Sadly enough, most runaway wives end up in neighborhood bars, work in humdrum jobs, and never meet anybody.

When do you hunt for a runaway parent and when do you let go? In cases where the runaway spouse has suffered unremitting physical and mental abuse, the attitude among counselors is to let go. In some cases, the spouses left behind feel that if they could only talk to the runaway things would be okay. Others would like to kill the runaway. Most just want alimony and child support.

What about finding a runaway mother or father? It can be as simple as talking to the runaway's own mother or father. Talk to the relatives, sympathize with the missing one, and in most cases they will tell you what they know. Usually the relatives know the whereabouts of the runaway.

You can file a missing persons report with the police, but no police department will send out an all-points bulletin or assign detectives to the case because it is not a crime to run away. Every person who is not a minor has the constitutional right to go where he wishes.

The exceptions are missing mentally retarded persons, missing persons over the age of sixty-five, or cases in which there is a suggestion of involuntary disappearance or the possibility of suicide.

Spouses have a constitutional right to run away, but they do not have the right to leave their children destitute. This is called abandonment, and it is a crime.

The Parent Locater Service is an investigative entity set up by the states to track down missing parents for support of their children. Statistics show that seventy-five percent of all absent parents live in the same state as the home they left.

What are the warning signs of a person's wanting to run away? In most cases the person will say that he or she intends to do so. He will tell others that he is unhappy with his life and wants a change.

In recent years the American family has been under enormous stress. Most families overextend themselves financially. Many husbands hold two jobs just to live paycheck to paycheck. About half of all mothers with children under eighteen are now working.

Everybody wants to be happy, wants the perfect life. The more we have, the more we want. We are never satisfied with our lot in life. Adults teach their children from an early age that the way to be happy is by accumulating material things. When the children grow up and discover how hard that is, they become bitter and want to quit, want to run.

Studies show that adults who ran away as children tend to be more emotionally disturbed, more given to heavy use of alcohol and drugs, and more prone to criminal behavior. Troubled kids run from troubled families into a troubled world that does not care what happens to them. Too many juvenile runaways become emotionally disturbed or unstable adults who raise a bunch of disturbed kids who become runaways.

What can we do? Look for early intervention for teenage runaways. Let's see how one teenage runaway, Kelly, solved her problems.

I have been running away all my life. From what I do not always know. But I just run. Oh, I have the "good" life, I guess you can say. My dad has a high-paying job with the city of Fort Worth. My mom sits at home all day and worries about the neighborhood gossip. I have one sister, Janey, who is fifteen. I'm seventeen. We get along pretty well. Janey is in trouble at school all the time. She can't do anything right. She skips classes, lies to the teachers, lies to Mom and Dad. But do you think they care? Heck, no. All Dad cares about is his precious job. And Mom, well, she should be a reporter for TV. All she does is get on that phone and gossip. I mean, I expect her to tell tales about herself one of these days.

You would think it would be Janey who runs away, but she is afraid of the dark. Well, I'm not. The first time I ran away I was thirteen. I stayed for a week over at a friend's house. Mom didn't even call about me for three days. That made me feel good! Janey said Dad didn't even miss me.

The second time I ran away I was fifteen. I went with this girl from school who had a lot of money she had stolen from her parents. We stayed in a nice hotel for two weeks until the money ran out. And then back home.

The last time I ran away was last year. For the first time I was really scared. I didn't have any place to go and was on the streets by myself. Some guys thought I was a hooker and followed me for three blocks. Finally I found this shelter in west Fort Worth. I found out later it was a shelter for battered women. They told me I could only stay for a week, then I had to leave. I went by my house, and Mom was having one of her little bridge parties. I saw her come outside, and she didn't look like she was upset; but I called one of my best friends, and she said Mom really was upset. Then I got to feeling guilty and went home.

Boy, was Dad mad! He said he had had enough. He took me to this family service agency where I met this lady counselor.

We talk three times a week. She is kinda nice, but she asks me a lot of personal questions that I get tired of answering. Dad has been staying home a lot more. Mom quit her bridge club and actually treats me and Janey like she loves us. Janey is improving in school by leaps and bounds.

Things were going great guns when Dad got laid off his job. Boy, things got bad around the house. He and Mom were yelling every morning. Then he found this other job and things are a lot better.

I'm supposed to talk to this counselor for about six months. She is really fun. She used to be a runaway too. It's not a great life, she said. I agree.

I'm also in this runaway recovery group at this service place. I've met a lot of nice kids who are just like me. When things get bad they want to run away. At least I'm not alone.

The counselor said I would always have this urge to run when I felt stressed, but I would have to learn to live with it. I think I'm going to be okay.

## WHERE TO GET HELP

Hot lines-1-800-231-6946

In Texas 1-800-392-3352

National Runaway Switchboard
1-800-621-4000

In Illinois
1-800-972-6004

Directory of Runaway Houses
National Youth Alternative Project
1346 Connecticut Avenue
Washington, DC 20036

Families Anonymous Inc.
P.O.Box 344
Torrance, CA 90501

# Just Between You
# and Your Stepfamily

S ome 13 percent of children under eighteen live with a remarried parent and a stepparent. Half a million adults become stepparents each year in the United States. Most children in stepfamilies are members of two households. The fact that "blended" families come from diverse backgrounds accentuates the need for tolerance.

With the rising rate of divorce and remarriage, more adults and children are living in stepfamilies, trying to cope with unique adjustment problems and stresses.

What are the problems encountered by stepfamilies? The same problems found in all family relationships: sibling rivalry, friction between parents and children, attempts by kids to play one parent against the other, disobedience, lack of understanding by spouse. Those problems, however, are more complicated because of the different structure of the stepfamily, and other problems arise just because of that unique structure.

One problem common to stepfamilies is the fact that there is a biological parent outside the stepfamily unit. Even when the natural parent has died, this absent parent continues to represent a strong psychological force within the family. Children usually think that the parent who is no longer with them was perfect and that the stepparent can never fill his or her shoes. Children and teens need to learn that they must accept the stepparent as a person and not compare him or her to the natural parent. Pictures of a dead spouse often hang in places of honor in the house even after a second marriage; this does not help the new spouse feel at home.

When the other parent is still alive, his or her power can be very great. If the relationship between the ex-spouses is amicable, cooperation can take place, but this good feeling can diminish when an ex-spouse remarries. Power struggles become all too common.

For example, a step family consisting of a wife and her two children and a husband and his three children has trouble forming good relationships because the ex-spouses insist on following visitation patterns set before the marriage. These visitation rights require the husband's kids to visit their mother every weekend and on holidays. That leaves the new stepmother, who works, little time to relax with her stepchildren. The new family has no time for fun activities.

Another stepfamily plans a vacation way ahead of time. Their plans are all set, and the luggage is packed. At the last minute the husband's ex-wife calls to says that she has decided to have the kids stay with her for the weekend instead of going on the vacation. This occurrence is very common and causes great emotional distress.

Another stepfamily problem is rules. One family has one set of rules, and the other family has another, totally different set. What is important in one household may not matter in the other household. The teen is confused.

What is the role of visiting stepchildren in the stepfamily? They are caught up in a no-win situation. They are not full members of the family, nor are they really visitors. This lack of clear roles and constant conflict of loyalties causes inner turmoil in the teenager.

Roles for stepparents are also not clearly defined. Stepparents do not know exactly what is expected of them, and other family members do not know what to expect of stepparents. For example, can a teacher expect a stepmother to come for a conference? Will a stepfather be called to the hospital when a teen is injured in an accident?

The fact that blended families come from such diverse backgrounds calls for great patience and understanding on everybody's part. Each family may have different values and needs, procedures and interactions. The families may have opposing religious beliefs, financial differences.

Steprelationships are new and untested. Say a couple have already established a relationship. Then suddenly here comes a teenager, a stepchild, which changes the picture entirely. In stepfamilies there is a sudden requirement that relationships be formed. Kids feel left out as their natural parents build their relationships with the stepchildren. Many teens discover that their new stepsiblings are not people they would choose as friends.

The most frequent cause of tension in stepfamilies is conflict over money. In stepfamilies, money can take on emotional overtones. There may be alimony payments to be made to an ex-spouse and child support money coming in from an ex-spouse. If the stepfamily income declines, the burden falls on the stepfamily; changes in the income of the ex-spouse do not mean that the alimony and child support stop. These are stressful areas.

Money is sometimes used as a weapon between ex-spouses. The constant exchange of money keeps them together and reliving hurtful feelings. A mother tells her daughter she can't have the prom dress she wants because her father does not give them enough money. An ex-wife receives a raise at work but keeps it secret from her ex-husband so he won't reduce his payments.

Past experiences in families and in former marriages influence feelings and behavior in the stepfamily. Some adults and teens find the stress of coping with stepfamilies too much to handle.

As a stepchild living in your second family, do you know when to get help? Look at these five warning signs:

## Feelings of constant anger

Of course you may feel anger in the initial adjustment period in your new situation, but why do you continue to feel anger? You may be angry at your parent for leaving you, or angry at the stepparent for taking away your special relationship with your natural parent. You may feel like part of a package deal that came with your parent's re-marriage. If after a full year of your parent's remarriage you still have hostile feelings, you should seek family counseling.

## Love and loyalty for your natural parents

Love may not happen instantly or even with effort between stepparent and stepchildren. You feel love and loyalty for your absent parent. Any cooperation with a stepparent may make you feel that you are showing less love for your natural parent.

## Guilt

Some teens believe they were the real cause of the divorce and family breakup and feel guilty. Or you may feel guilty for not being able to love the stepparent.

## Loss and mourning

Feelings of loss and mourning are expected at the breakup of a family from divorce or death. There may be feelings of loss of the original family. If your stepparent treats you better than your natural parent, it can bring loss of another kind—loss of what could have been between you and that parent in the future.

## Fear

After you have experienced the loss of a parent through death or divorce, you have constant fears that it could happen again. Stepparents and stepchildren fear that the new parent will not be as good at it as the natural one.

How can you live better and more happily with your stepfamily? Read and discuss these suggestions with your family and put some in practice.

- It is difficult to have a new person in the family, and it is difficult to be the new person in a family. Cut down on feelings involved with "territory." It helps if families can start out in a new house or apartment.
- Forming new relationships within the stepfamily can be important, especially if you are young. Do

things together with your new family. For example, stepfather and children can plant a garden together. Stepmother and daughter can go shopping together. Activities help relationships grow and develop.

- It is helpful to preserve original relationships, for a parent and natural kids to have time together.
- Caring and good relationships take time. Not everything is instant in life. Try to develop things at your own comfortable pace.
- Accept that a stepfamily is a new type of family. It too can be enjoyable and have opportunities for growth.
- Teenagers will always have a definite pull toward their biological parents. Rejection of a stepparent may have nothing to do with him or her personally.
- A courteous relationship between ex-spouses is important. Although difficult to maintain, if at all possible it should be worked out. In that way the kids are not caught up between the parents and have no need to take sides. Direct contact between the adults is best since it does not place the children in the position of being carriers.
- Children as well as adults have a family history. Much can be gained by coming together to work out new family patterns. Many solutions can be found with time and patience.
- Being a stepparent is an unclear task and at times difficult. Each family member should have a role to play.
- Discipline is not usually accepted by stepchildren until a friendly relationship has been established, which is often a matter of a year and a half to two years. Both adults need to support each other's authority in the household. Usually the natural parent

is the main person to discipline; but if the natural parent is not around, the stepparent should have the authority. The parents must work together.

- Integrating a stepfamily with teenagers is almost impossible, difficult at best. Teenagers are trying to move away from their families in any type of family. In single-parent families teenagers have often been young adults, and with the remarriage of a parent they may find it hard to return to being treated as a child again. Teenagers have more of a family history than younger children and sometimes withdraw from the new family.

- Visiting children usually feel strange and like outsiders in the new neighborhood. It is helpful if they have some place in the house that they can call their own private space. Should they be included in family chores? Yes.

- Parents who don't have full custody of the children find it hard to instill their family values when they have so little time with them. But kids learn from watching the other family members and how they interact with each other. It may take time before they decide to join in the activities.

- You may become more aware of sexuality in a stepfamily because you are living with people whom you did not grow up with. It is vital that the kids receive affection from both parents. Parents need to explain any sexual attraction the teens may feel for one another or for the adults.

- All families experience stress at one time or another. Teens and adults need to show day-to-day appreciation of each of other. Stepfamilies are families of loss, and feelings can be especially intense—feelings such as jealousy, rejection, guilt, anger. Try to be realistic about your expectations, and that will reduce your disappointments.

- Try to keep good contact between adults and teens. Communication skills are vital to closer understanding.

Marriage is not going out of style. Eighty percent of divorced persons remarry. Sixty percent of them have children. And those children have children and raise them according to their own upbringing.

What can you do as a stepfamily wanting to grow, wanting to have a positive family atmosphere? Any family having problems should consider counseling and therapy.

Therapeutic approaches that are used with stepfamilies include individual therapy, couples, groups, and family counseling. Workshops and lectures on stepfamilies are given. Books and articles about stepparents are published, which help stepparents see that they are not alone with their problems.

Let's see how Lori handled her new stepfamily.

My name is Lori and I'm fourteen. My parents got divorced last year, and boy, were we glad. All they did was argue and graph and throw things. Most kids are upset when their parents split up, but not me and my brother. I'd rather live in a rabbit hutch than with my parents constantly arguing.

It was my mom who left my dad. She told me the night before that she was leaving Dad for good. She said she had a new boyfriend, and he was a lot better to her than Dad. I'm glad it was dark in the car when she told me, because I felt tears slip down my cheeks. I was sad and glad at the same time.

Mom told Dad the next day after supper. He was

upset. He called her a lot of nasty names and then stormed out of the house. Mom was crying. My brother went out and left me there without even asking if I wanted to go. I was mad at him, mad at Dad, and mad at Mom. Why couldn't we be a normal family like everyone else?

My stomach hurt all night. And even though I had known they would eventually give up on each other, I thought it was pretty sad. I mean, a part of me doesn't give a flip if they divorce or not. Then there is a part of me that really cares. So Mom and Dad made up, so we thought, and life went on as usual. Then one day I came in from school on a normal, average day, and Mom and Dad dropped the bomb. They were getting a divorce. Just like that. A twenty-two-year marriage ended on a winter day. My brother was really upset. He went out and got drunk that night like a fool. I went with Dad for a long drive, and he explained to me that Mom had found another man. Mom had found a man that she loved more than him. I thought he was going to cry, but he didn't. We stopped to get some ice cream, and he changed the subject completely. Just like that. I was never supposed to ask how Mom met this man or anything.

The divorce was final in two months. Dad moved out that weekend. Mom helped him pack. It was really weird. Then after Dad left Mom sat down and had a good cry. Then she wiped her eyes, called her new boyfriend, and they went out on a date.

I could not believe my eyes when I first saw Mom's new boyfriend. He is ugly. Dad is a lot better looking. This new guy is short, balding, and a little fat. But you should see the way he treats Mom. Wow!

When he came to the door he had a bunch of

flowers in a vase. He kissed Mom a long kiss on the lips and walked in and hugged her. I nearly threw up. Mom just glowed like a teenager. Night after night this man came to pick up Mom. My brother would not even talk to him. He said hi to me one night and smiled. He was kinda cute when he smiled.

The day before school started that next year Mom said this man Robert wanted to take me and my brother out to dinner. Believe it or not, my brother said fine, and we went to dinner with Robert.

Robert was very nice and polite. I caught my brother even laughing a little. Robert announced that he and Mom were getting married. He said he really loved her. He said he wanted us to be a happy family and that he had never had kids before. Robert said he would do anything in the world for Mom and for us.

The next week he and Mom were married in a quiet ceremony at the house. I have to admit I have never seen Mom happier than she was that day.

Robert moved in with us and put his clothes in Dad's closet as if he had always belonged there and not Dad. It was so strange. Me and my brother were used to Mom and Dad fighting all the time, but all Robert and Mom do is kiss and hug, and it's nice.

Robert is going to take my brother hunting and fishing. He is going to take me shopping. He is super nice to us. But poor Dad. Dad still comes to see us once a week, and he looks so miserable. I told him he ought to find a girlfriend. He just laughed. He said he was still in love with Mother.

# CHAPTER 7

# When Your Parents

# Divorce

O ne out of two marriages ends in divorce, a startling but true fact of life in the United States today. Why? Today men and women have fewer concrete criteria by which to measure a prospective spouse. The fact that a man makes a good living is no longer a sign that he will make a good husband. What about a man's interest in having children? What about a woman's eagerness to work and contribute to the family's income as a sign of her devotion? Rules of a solid relationship can be made only in general terms.

Today's couples have to depend more than ever on their own feelings. Married couples need to share their inner-most thoughts, their problems and burdens, and to be compatible companions. How do they go about doing this? By trial and error, by feeling their own way, making mistakes, and learning to tolerate both being hurt and hurting. They need to talk over grievances, to be reasonable in the heat of anger, and to be forgiving and understanding in the many disappointments of life.

If couples are going to marry for love, they need to be sure they can reverse the situation if they later find that they have made a mistake.

What are a couple's expectations of marriage? What does each partner want and expect from the other and the marriage vows? Discuss your expectations before you marry. Don't find out after it is too late.

What kind of marriage do your parents have? What kind is most likely to end? Let's look at seven types of marriage.

## THE LOVING MARRIAGE

In the beginnng as two people date they develop a warm companionship and friendship. During the courtship and marriage both reveal themselves in times of crisis and of peace. They have a healthy respect for each other, knowing their differences as well as their similarities. They experience conflicts, but not to see who is right and who is wrong. Love is given freely and not possessively. Each finds joy in the other's success. Noncompetitive, their relationship is vital and lively. Each depends on each other but can also stand alone. The decision to have children is made together out of love.

It has been said that it takes a long time to learn to love well, where as it takes only a few months to become embittered, depressed. A good marriage takes work and study.

## THE ANTAGONISTIC MARRIAGE

The man and wife are miserable with each other but cannot let go. They constantly play dirty pool with each other. Each partner sees the other merely as an object on which to gratify his or her own needs. There may be verbal and physical violence, aloofness, and periods of hot and cold. If the couple remain married it is largely out of fear of not being married. The presence of children usually deepens the antagonism but is seen as a reason to stay married.

## THE FRIENDLY MARRIAGE

This couple get along because it is more convenient to remain married than to break up an emotionally meager relationship. Being married has its social, economic, and sexual advantages. This is the modern version of the old-fashioned arranged marriage. It is the live-and-let-live marriage. Husband and wife have their own careers and usually high incomes.

## THE STATIC MARRIAGE

These partners remain compatible as long as no one rocks the boat or changes. Both husband and wife have their well-defined roles. One is usually dominant in relation to the other. The husband may be father to the wife, or husband and wife may treat each other as siblings. The one thing that upsets the entire balance is the birth of a child, which may turn the marriage into an antagonistic type.

## THE CYCLICAL MARRIAGE

The couple go through periods of sharp disagreements followed by periods of serenity and joy. Their fights and arguments reach each other and bring about change at a cost of personal distress. When they are happy, they are very happy. When they are sad, they are very sad. There are no in-between feelings in this marriage. As the partners age, these marriages may become more loving and show less friction.

## THE ROMANTIC MARRIAGE

This is the love-at-first-sight union, the passionate courtship followed by the hangover after the honeymoon. One or both partners become disillusioned, saying the other one fooled them.

Whatever kind of marriage your parents have or had, any of of them can fail at any time. What is the best way to live through your parents' divorce? It is vital for the children to understand the emotional climate of life in divorce. If old enough, the children should discuss certain matters with their parents as they divorce: Who has custody rights? What are the visitation rights? Who keeps the house? What about financial support? What about health care? These and other important questions should be discussed with both parents.

Let's look at Terri's story and how she handled her parents' divorce.

I still cannot believe my parents are divorced. They split up four years ago, and I still cannot get used to the fact. You see, my family is not the kind of family that is supposed to divorce. My mother comes from a wealthy family. She has never had to live without what she wanted. When she saw Dad in a college class her first year away from home, she wanted him too. At first he didn't seem to be interested in her, but she made sure she was in every class of his, and eventually he got the hint. They dated for about three years and then got married. Now, my father did not come from a wealthy family. It didn't take him long after the expensive, lavish wedding to see that he had married into money. He decided from the first that he would make something of himself using Mom's family money. Well, Mom didn't care. After all, she loved him dearly and he was her husband, so she could trust him. Right? Wrong.

It didn't take Dad long to run through quite a bunch of the money. He quit his job and wanted to own a tire store. The franchise alone cost a million dollars, and just to build the store was another fifty thousand. But Dad did not build the store where they told him to. He built it on the wrong side of town. In six months the store was closed, and the money was down the drain. Did Mom care or know what was going on? She was too busy having my two older sisters and me.

Dad's next adventure was a men's clothing store. Here again, just to buy the name cost a fortune. Mom kept telling Dad that he had too much competition in the mall downtown. Did dad listen? No. This store started out great, but soon the mall and its grand scale of advertising and cutthroat prices had put Dad and his store out of business again.

By this time my sisters and I were growing up. Mom and Dad argued constantly. Dad began to drink and run around with other women. But Mom was stuck with three kids, so she stayed with Dad and put up with his bad business deals, drinking, and other women.

The years flew by. My sisters married, and I was left alone to hear Mom and Dad's fights getting worse and worse. He started hitting both of us. I think I spent half my time in my room with the door locked.

It got really bad, but Mom would never get help. By my senior year in high school, home life was unbearable. I was determined to get away at any cost.

I married Randy the night of graduation. I loved Randy, but I loved even more getting away from Dad.

It didn't take me long to realize that I had made a serious mistake with Randy. He was a lot like Dad: mean, hateful, selfish. And he drank and ran around with other women. I thought I was going to have a nervous breakdown at one point. All those years with Dad and now Randy. I had jumped from the frying pan into the fire.

Mom and I filed for divorce the same day! Then we went to lunch and celebrated. Mom still had a little money; we would live together on that and go to college for a degree. Life had to get better for us, and it did.

Mom is studying for a business degree. I'm studying journalism. We share a small two-bedroom apartment. My sisters were luckier than I. For one thing they got away before Dad got real bad, and also they found good husbands right from the start. Maybe someday Mom and I will have good marriages.

## SUGGESTED READING

A *Marriage Manual*
Hannah and Abraham Stone
Simon and Schuster, New York

*The Happy Family*
John and Ruth Munroe
Alfred A. Knopf, New York

*Predicting Adjustment in Marriage*
J.H.Locke
Holt, Rinehart & Winston, New York

*American Marriage and Divorce*
Paul H. Jacobson
Holt, Rinehart & Winston, New York

*The Divorce Handbook*
Florence Haussaman, Mary Guitar
G.P. Putnam's Sons, New York

*After Divorce*
William Goode
Free Press, New York

*Children of Divorce*
Louise Despert
Doubleday, Co., New York.

# CHAPTER 8

# When Your
# Parents Work

T he typical schoolchild today lives with two em-
ployed parents. Why? Most mothers and fathers
work because it is an economic necessity. Maintaining a family is expensive. A researcher at Ohio State
University has estimated that the average middle-class
two-parent family setting out to raise a child in 1990 can
expect to spend about $140,000 to age twenty-three. The
estimate for a lower-income family is about $70,000. The
money is for food, clothing, housing, medical bills, and
school supplies and does not cover a college education.

Some children find the two-job situation has benefits
that have nothing to do with material goods. These teens
understand the relationship between the level of income
and the level of family stress. They say it is better for both
parents to work than to hear them argue over money matters all the time and to worry about their divorcing. The
stress that comes from facing heavy financial demands is

clearly eased in most homes when the mother works. Even younger children have a sense of the role money plays in maintaining a stable home atmosphere.

Teens and smaller children want to understand what their parents do at work. When parents talk about their jobs, children get a mental image of how they spend their working hours. In a survey of fourth through twelfth graders, 87 percent knew what their fathers did for a living and 83 percent knew what their mothers did. Between 25 and 30 percent could not describe their parents' jobs.

Do you feel that your parents spend too much time at work? Eight out of ten teens interviewed believed that their parents placed more importance on being a good employee than on being a good parent. They said their parents always have something that must be done for work, that they stay late at work and work on weekends. What can you do about it? What are the three major problems of working families?

## COMMUNICATION

Keep an open line of communication with your parents. Teens in homes where mothers and fathers work have fewer opportunities to communicate with them. If you want to have a good relationship with your parents you have to talk to them. Plan time just to talk to your Mom and Dad. Many parents are so busy with their own lives that they forget their most important jobs—their children.

Over half of the children surveyed aged thirteen and under who are at home alone for more than two hours a day reported that their father never talks to them. Teens and smaller children who are at home alone for the longest period of time and have the greatest need of verbal support are least likely to receive support from their father. Sixty percent of teens are able to get their father's attention and support.

Overall, teens give their mothers higher ratings in their ability to listen. After work, mothers make a greater effort to communicate with their children. What do teens want to talk about to their parents? They want to talk about being scared when they are alone, having much responsibility at home, failing in school. Teens also want to talk about serious subjects such as sex, drugs, God, religion, and death. Only 40 percent of fathers and 50 percent of mothers talk to their kids about serious subjects. Whom do you talk to if your parents won't listen? Try a close relative, a good teacher, a school counselor. But find someone to answer your questions. Don't find out the hard way.

## CRITICISM

If this is the only kind of communication you have with your parents, the bond between you can be irreparably damaged. Conversation filled with criticism is not conversation but a sparring match. There is no winner. Here are ten tips for better talk with your parents.

1. Willingly stop any activity to talk with your parent.
2. Set aside time for each parent.
3. Focus attention on your parent's words, tone of voice, and body language.
4. Allow your parent to choose the topic of discussion.
5. Let your parent have an opportunity to dominate the conversation.
6. Express understanding and sympathy.

7. Respect your parent's point of view, and don't evaluate feelings or opinions.
8. Maintain eye contact. Don't look away.
9. Sit physically close to your parent.
10. Relax and enjoy the conversation.

## TELEPHONING

The first thing you should do when you get home from school is to call your parents. Call at least one parent to say that you are safe and sound. It is good to hear their voices when you come home to an empty house. The telephone is a vital tool for families with two working parents.

The afternoon telephone call fulfills an important emotional function. After a long day your parent wants to hear what happened at school, about the 100 you made on that important spelling test, about the boy you like who has finally asked you for a date. You especially need to talk to them if you have had a rough day—your English teacher chewed you out for cheating but you didn't cheat, you were moved to last chair in the band, your best friend stole your boyfriend. We all have days like that, and it helps to talk to the people who love you the most—your parents.

The arrangements you make for daily telephone calls should be clear to you and your parents. It may be easier for you to call your parents at work, but there should be clear rules about that. If your parent has a job where you can't call, make arrangements to call your grandmother or a close friend when you get home.

What are some things you can do to make your working family a happier household?

- *Make the morning the best time* you spend with your parents. That time sets the tone of your day. Some teens get up early with their parents and have light talk or make plans for the afternoon. Having something to took forward to can help both you and your parent get through the day with a smile.

• *Share responsibility.* Everyone in the family should have a job to do when both parents work. It is too much to expect your mother to do all the housework when she has worked all day. You might have a household chore checklist hung where it can be seen to remind everyone of their duties.

• *Visit your parent's workplace.* This can be fun. If possible, visit where both your parents work. You can learn a lot about them that way.

• *Follow study rules:*

1. Allot a specific time period every day for homework.
2. Keep a separate pad or notebook for recording all assignments.
3. Mark on a calendar the dates when work is due.
4. Choose a work place away from distractions.
5. Keep pencils, papers, dictionary, and other school materials in a designated place.
6. Organize!
7. Keeps tabs on long-term assignments so that the work is done at a steady pace and not in a last-minute rush.

You and your parents should discuss ways of making your home safe while you are there alone after school. Following are some idea to discuss:

1. Have an alarm system installed.
2. Lock all windows and doors. Nearly half of all

burglaries occur when someone has failed to lock a door or window.

3. Have a key for each member of the family.
4. Install a phone answering machine for last-minute changes of plans.
5. Keep a radio on if you hate to come into an empty house.
6. Cut back shrubbery that could conceal a person.
7. Do not leave ladders and tools outside.
8. Do not display the family name on the mailbox.
9. Close garage doors.
10. Do not leave notes on doors or windows.
11. Do not leave outside lights on during the day.

## FACING EMERGENCIES

All of us at one time or another will face an emergency. Every year 14,000 children lose their lives because of accidents, and twenty-three million children under sixteen years of age are seriously hurt. Accidents are the leading cause of death among teenagers in the United States.

Emergency numbers of doctors, fire department, hospital emergency room, and neighbors should be posted next to the telephone. Some emergencies require immediate attention. You should call the doctor RIGHT AWAY if you or a sibling or friend:

1. Has a cut with profuse or continued bleeding.
2. Has swallowed a poisonous substance such as the wrong medicine, rubbing alcohol, bleach, or a detergent.
3. Has a broken bone or a joint injury.
4. Has an eye or ear injury.

5. Has been burned or scalded.
6. Begins to choke or finds it hard to breathe.
7. Has been bitten by a dog, cat, snake, scorpion, bee, or other animal or insect.
8. Feels lightheaded, dizzy, or as if losing consciousness.

**Gas.**   An undetected gas leak can cause a major explosion that could reduce your home to a pile of rubble. If you smell gas, open the windows and doors. If the odor is strong, leave the house immediately and call the gas company from a neighbor's house. If you feel sick or nauseated, call a doctor.

**Storms.**   Do not leave the house in a bad storm. Bring all pets inside. In an electrical storm, stay away from single trees and flagpoles and towers.

**Fire.**   A smoldering flame can produce fumes that can suffocate you. If you see or smell smoke or hear a smoke detector, go to a neighbor's house and call the fire department. If your clothes catch on fire, DO NOT RUN. Lie down and roll back and forth until the flames are out. If you are outside, roll in the dirt and sand. Your family should draw up an emergency fire plan with two escape routes in case one is blocked by fire. Practic that escape plan. Have fire detectors and fire extinguishers in your home.

## UNKNOWN PHONE CALLS

The phone can be a blessing and a curse. It is scary to answer the phone when you are alone and find no one on the line, or the person says something scary or nasty to you. HANG UP if the caller becomes vulgar. Blow a sharp whistle in the phone to hurt the ear of the caller. If the calls continue, notify the police. Such calls are illegal, and the phone company along with the police can trace them. You do not have to give information to a stranger. NEVER tell a stranger calling that you are home alone; say that your parents are in the garage or in the shower.

## UNEXPECTED VISITORS

Caution is the word when dealing with unknown people at your door. If the doorbell rings, look out a peephole in the door or out the window. NEVER answer the door without looking first. If you do not know the person, do not open the door. Here are some life-saving tips for unwanted visitors:

- Never admit a stranger.
- Do not tell anyone that no adult is home.
- Do not open the door a few inches on the chain.
- Do not open the door for delivery people or a repairman.
- Do not open the door for a stranger whose car has broken down.

## INTRUDERS IN YOUR HOME

If you come home from school and notice that something is wrong or different, do not go in. Go to a neighbor and call the police.

Here are three tips if you surprise an intruder:

1. Avoid any confrontation with the intruder. He may react violently when he is surprised.

2. Be passive. Do not try to capture him. Let him leave alone.
3. Get help immediately. As soon as it is safe, call the police and describe the intruder.

Let's see how Michelle, age fifteen, handles being alone after school while her parents work.

I like being home most of the time. Both of my parents work, and I know they have to, so I don't complain although I do get lonely sometimes. School is out at three, and I walk home with friends. I may visit some friends down the street until about four-thirty, when they have to go in. Then I'm home alone until about six-thirty when my parents come home.

It's not too bad. I call Mom when I walk in the door. I tell her about my day and she tells me about hers. Then I get a snack and watch TV. If I don't visit friends, I read or listen to music. I keep the doors locked and feel pretty safe. I did get scared once when a man I didn't know came to the door and kept ringing the bell. I just sat quietly until he went away. I've gotten a few strange phone calls, but they never call back.

I'm an only child, so I get a lot of nice things since Mom works. We always have something planned to do when she gets off. Being alone allows me to do just what I want to do. For example, I like to write stories. After I do my homework and feed my dog Scooter, I try to do some writing. It's easy because it's very quiet in the house.

When Mom and Dad get home my writing comes to a halt. We decide where we want to eat or if we want to eat at home. After dinner we talk and pick out a video movie at the store if there is not a good movie on television.

On Friday nights Mom and Dad go out dancing. I can have a girlfriend over to spend the night, or I can spend the night at somebody's house. Saturday is Mom's and my day to ourselves. We eat out, shop at the mall, catch a movie, or whatever we feel like. Sometimes we visit my grandparents in a neighboring town.

Sure, there are times when I get lonely, but for the most part I love having some privacy. I have a lot of cousins who live about 20 miles away, and I visit them on weekends. They are around my age, and we like the same music, the same clothes, and stuff. It's fun being with them, but after a while I want to be alone again so I can write or read.

To me, having working parents means that your parents love you enough to work and give you the best kind of life they can. It's up to you to do your part and make the best of it.

# CHAPTER 9

# Suicide

**J**enny Martin could stand her life no longer. With a single shot to her head she killed herself one Sunday morning. Why? Why would a beautiful sixteen-year-old like Jenny end her brief life? Eighteen teenagers a day kill themselves. Every 80 minutes another teenager commits suicide, according to the National Institute of Mental Health.

What are the reasons? Peer pressure, divorced parents, being overweight, feeling left out of the group at school, drug abuse, unwanted pregnancy, alcoholism. The list goes on and on. What can we do as a nation, what can you do as one person to help stop these senseless tragedies?

Suicide is America's second-largest killer. Over one hundred teens a week kill themselves. In a year's time the total comes to a staggering 6,500 lives lost. Add to that the number of people directly affected by suicides—parents, family, members friends, classmates. Those left behind are perplexed and grieving. They are left with the burning question, WHY?

It is estimated that over a thousand teenagers try unsuccessfully to kill themselves every day, almost one a

minute. Many of the attempts are not intended to succeed; they are cries for help. But even so, thousands of
teens permanently maim themselves in botched attempts.

Many coroners will not rule a death a suicide if no note is
left. Only a small percentage of suicides leave anything in
writing. On many death certificates suicide is diguised,
to protect insurance benefits or to shield a family from
embarrassment. In our society a stigma is placed on
suicide.

Let's look at the main reasons teens commit suicide:

## LONELINESS

In a home with two wage-earners, teens get to spend little
time with their parents. They have not just less quality
time, but less quantity time. Less time means less guidance.

## DRUGS

A recent *Weekly Reader* survey of the drug scene reported
that 39 percent of fourth graders said that using drugs is a
big problem. Teens and young kids use drugs to fit in. Of
students interviewed, 76 percent usually buy drugs from
other students, and 14 percent buy from a dealer near
school; 36 percent were first offered drugs at ages twelve to
fifteen. Among youth twelve to seventeen 12 percent are
regular pot users. Forty-two percent of high school seniors
smoked pot during the year and stayed stoned an average
of three hours each time. By the end of high school, two
thirds of American teenagers have used illicit drugs. Teens
will do anything to get high, sniff gas or glue, inhale aerosol
spray.

Teenager, watch out for drugs. They are a never-ending
nightmare. Be smart. Say NO to drugs.

## PREGNANCY

With an estimated 11.6 million teenagers now sexually active, a few schools have begun dispensing birth control devices and establishing day-care facilities for students. The research organization known as SIECUS (Sex Information and Education Council of the United States) reports that one of every two boys age fifteen to seventeen has had sex. Nearly half of girls fifteen to nineteen years old have had sex and one of every two is sexually active. The National Center for Health Statistics reports that only one in five women waits for marriage to have sex.

Sexual activity among teens leads to pregnancy, which leads to abortion. Almost half of teenage girls who become pregant have abortions, which accounts for a third of all abortions in the United States. Abortion seems to be most common among the affluent; upper-middle-class girls view it as a means of birth control.

It is estimated that 40 percent of today's fourteen-year-old girls will become pregnant at least once before they are twenty. The United States has the highest incidence of teenage motherhood in any Western country, 52 per thousand as compared with 32 per thousand in Great Britain. Two out of three pregnant girls drop out of school.

Nearly half of the black females in the U.S. become pregnant by age twenty, and 90 percent of black babies are born out of wedlock; most are raised in fatherless homes.

## ALCOHOL

Betty and Barbara were stopped at a traffic light. A flashy sports car eased up beside them, and Betty caught a glimpse of the handsome guy driving the car. She lowered her window and started a conversation.

Before long the man invited Betty and Barbara to have drinks with him. The girls met him at a tavern and had drinks. After a while they strolled down the beach, still drinking. Finally the man asked Betty to drive home with him, so Barbara followed in her car. Barbara said the man must have been going 80 miles an hour when there was a spectular crash and he ran head-on into the oncoming cars. Barbara ran to the accident to help Betty, but it was too late. Her friend was burned beyond recognition.

It happens at least 23,000 times a year when the combination of alcohol and an automobile results in death. Two and a half million people are maimed for life as a result of auto accidents. Drinking and driving is the number one teen killer; it kills eight thousand teenagers a year.

Surveys cited by the National Council on Alcoholism report that 30 percent of the nation's nine-year-olds feel pressured to drink. Today there are 3.3 million teenage alcoholics in the United States; that's one in every nine teens! A teenage alcoholic, like any alcoholic, commits slow suicide. The body is damaged and the life span is reduced.

## ROCK AND ROLE MODELS

There is no question that the life-styles, philosophies, and lyrics of some rock stars are a damaging influence on American youth. Here are some examples of song lyrics that deal with death and suicide:

- AC/DC's "Shoot to Thrill" tells listeners to pull the trigger for a super thrill.
- "Kill Yourself to Live" by Black Sabbath is a ballad of hopelessness and despair.

- Blue Oyster Cult's video "I'm Burning for You" shows a young man who kills himself by setting his car on fire. This group also produced "Don't Fear the Reaper," which describes a suicide pact between two lovers.
- The group Loverboy sings "Teenage Overdose."
- The Pet Shop Boys perform a video that shows a gun pointed to the head. The song "West End" tells listeners they are better off dead.

The best-known of all the controversial songs is Ozzy Osbourne's "Suicide Solution." The lyrics describe the life of a boy locked inside his house from a horrible world. After listening to Osbourne's albums for several hours, John McCollum, nineteen, killed himself with one shot from his father's pistol.

## UNHAPPY HOME LIFE

One of the most common reasons for teenage suicide is an unhappy home life. The breakdown of family life is the chief area of concern in seeking answers to the teenage suicide epidemic. Most teenage suicides occur at home, and most have their origin at home. Instead of peace at home, there is fear. Instead of harmony, there is discord. Many suicides have no connection with drugs or alcohol. What are some problems in the home today?

- Divorce: In 1980 one in every thirty-six marriages ended in divorce.
- Remarriage: Replacing an original parent where there is no bond of love with a stepmother or stepfather is impossible for many teens.
- Blended families: 17 percent of remarriages that

involve stepchildren on both sides wind up in divorce within three years.
- Single-parent families: 12.6 million children under the age of eighteen live with only one parent.
- Undeclared divorce: Homes in which the parents are together legally but not emotionally.
- The trauma of transition: The average American family moves every three years. It's not always easy for teens to make new friends and adjust.
- Child abuse: One million children and teens are abused each year.

The home can be a breeding ground for suicidal thoughts. Teenagers should keep open lines of communication with parents.

## PEER PRESSURE

There is no pressure like teen pressure these days. A professor of psychiatry at the University of Pennsylvania, asked what kind of person commits suicide, cited people who have a negative self-image or have gone through severe stress such as a disappointment in a career or a relationship. A temperament that could lead to suicide can be inherited.

Broken dreams top the list of reasons for teenage suicide. Some kids don't have the natural talent they crave; some girls are not pretty enough to become models.

Broken romances are high on the list. Many teenagers feel that when a romance is over life isn't worth living.

Broken expectations hurt when a best friend lets you down or steals your boyfriend.

Broken hearts are the hardest blows of all, such as the death of a loved one.

## MENTAL ILLNESS

The saddest reason of all for suicide is mental illness. Teens who are depressed for a long period of time need to get professional help. If your parents won't help you, find an adult who will.

What are some signs of suicidal thoughts? Kids who are normally outgoing become moody and silent. Kids who usually make good grades start failing in school. They become withdrawn and constantly depressed. They may become aggressive, picking fights with everybody. Some fall victim to eating disorders, eating too much or too little. Some teens who are thinking of suicide may suddenly start giving away prized possessions. Some threaten suicide, telling everyone, "I'm going to kill myself."

What can you do to stop a friend from killing himself? First of all, don't back away. Listen to him. Keep a lookout for possible problems. Tell a trusted adult if a friend says he is going to kill himself.

Let's read one girl's story of her sister Becky who killed herself.

Becky was beautiful, smart, and had it all. Then why did she drive her car off a California cliff? Why would the head cheerleader of a Los Angeles high school end her life? My sister Becky was dating the football quarterback, the best-looking guy in the school. She had friends, she had a sports car, she had the best clothes. But Becky was not happy.

What did Becky want? What was missing in her life? Our mother had a drinking problem. Not real bad, but bad enough to make our life miserable. Dad made lots of money, so Mother never worked, she never knew what it was like trying to live from paycheck to paycheck. I think she was just bored to death. She had no challenge in life, no goal. All she did was think about herself, what she wanted, when she wanted, how she wanted.

I remember the day Becky came in crying, upset that her first boyfriend was moving out of town. Becky went out to the pool where Mom was having her usual afternoon cocktail, and Mom just shrugged it off. Well, it was a big deal to Becky. I mean, her heart was broken.

Then there was the time Becky wanted Mom to be there when she tried out for cheerleader. Mom said she would show up, but she didn't; she thought a tennis match was more important. Thank goodness Becky was elected cheerleader, but she was still disappointed in Mom.

Dad tried to do things for us, but he was out of town a lot with his job. Becky and I begged Dad to get help for Mom, but he always said no.

I think the last straw for Becky was the time she thought she was pregnant. She came home hysterical, and as usual Mom was out by the pool fading away. When Becky told her about her problem, all Mom did was to calmly write her a check for an abortion. Just like that. No questions, no nothing. As it turned out, Becky was not pregnant, but she never forgave Mom for her attitude.

I was away at college when Dad called with the news of Becky's death. I was devastated. The car had plunged hundreds of feet and caught on fire. I couldn't believe Becky would hurt her pretty face.

Two years after Becky's death, Dad finally got Mom

to go to an alcoholism clinic. Mom really changed after Becky's death. I just think it's sad that she didn't change *before* Becky died.

I will always love and miss my sister. I will remember her happy and laughing.

# CHAPTER 10

# Living with a

# Battered Parent

One of every two women in the United States will be the victim of a violent encounter with her husband at some time in her life.

What is husband abuse? What is battering? The list includes beating, hitting, shoving, pinching, verbal abuse, and mental abuse.

The long-term effects of battering can be so pervasive that it's sometimes hard to pinpoint exactly how the abuse affects you as a teenager and your battered mother. It permeates everything: your sense of self, your intimate relationships, your sexuality, your parenting, your work, even your sanity. Everywhere you look, you see its effects.

Many battered mothers have been too busy surviving to notice the ways you were hurt by this abuse. But you cannot heal until you acknowledge the areas that need healing.

How your battered parent handles the abuse has a lot to do with the impact on you. If you are met with compassion, healing begins immediately; but if no one notices your pain, or if you are blamed or not believed, the damage is compounded.

Not all survivors are affected in the same ways. You may do well in one area in your life, but not in another. You may succeed in school, but not in your relationships. Some teenagers have a nagging sense that something is wrong. For others, the damage is so extensive that they feel they've wasted their whole lives.

Relationships are distorted in battered families. The essential trust, sharing, and safety are missing, and in their place are secrecy, isolation, and fear. If you were abused by a family member or saw your mother being abused, you may have been made the family scapegoat. You may have been told repeatedly that you are bad and crazy. You may feel isolated, cut off from contact with others. Where are you now?

- Are you satisfied with your family relationships?
- Do people in your family support you?
- Do you feel crazy or depressed when you see your father?
- Have you confronted your father?
- Do you feel safe with your father?
- Do you expect your father to change?
- Does the battering continue in your family?

How can you and your battered parent start to heal? The healing process is a continuum. It begins with the experience of surviving, an awareness of the fact that you have lived through the abuse and made it this far. It ends with thriving, the experience of a satisfying life no longer programmed by what happened to you as a child growing up.

Healing is not a random process. All survivors pass through definite stages, although not necessarily in the same order.

The healing process is like a spiral. You may go through the same stage over and over. You may spend a year on the same stage. With each new cycle, your capacity to feel, to remember is strengthened.

Although most of these stages are necessary for every survivor, a few of them—the emergency stage, remembering the abuse, confronting your family, and forgiveness— are not necessarily applicable to every person.

## THE DECISION TO HEAL

1. Accept the fact of the abuse. Find help dealing with it.
2. The emergency stage—deal with memories.
3. Remember—try to remember as far back as you can.
4. Believe it happened—don't doubt yourself.
5. Trust yourself—listen to your own inner voice.
6. Grieve and mourn—grieving is a way to honor your pain.
7. Feel anger, the backbone of healing—direct your anger at the abuser.
8. Confront your battered parent. This is not advised for every family, but it can be a dramatic release and a healing tool.
9. Forgive. Forgiving the abuser is not an essential part of the healing process, but it is recommended. Do forgive yourself and your battered parent.
10. Seek spirituality through religion. Having a sense of a power greater than yourself can help in the healing process.

11. Make resolutions and move on—come to terms with your battered parent and your abuser parent. While you can't go back and change your life history, you can make lasting changes in your life and gain the power to work through your feelings.

Healing is not easy. Choosing to work on healing will raise questions you didn't want to ask and answers you didn't want to hear. Your life will never be the same. Deciding to heal is terrifying because it means opening up hope. For many battered families, hope has brought only disappointment.

What can you do right now to survive your battered home?

- Don't hurt yourself. You deserve to live.
- Know that you're not going crazy.
- Find people to talk to.
- Get professional help.
- Get support from other survivors.
- Do as many nice things for yourself as you can.
- Drop what isn't essential in your life.
- Find or create a safe area in your house or find a place to go when things get bad. You do not have to stay and watch physical or mental abuse. Get help for your Mom and LEAVE.
- Get out of abusive situations on a job or at school. You have enough stress at home without adding any more.
- Remind yourself that you *are* going to live through this.
- Develop a belief in something other than yourself.
- Remember, this too shall pass.

## LIVING WITHOUT VIOLENCE

There is a difference between anger and violence. Anger is an emotion, and violence is one of the behaviors that can express that emotion. Many people do not know they are angry until they reach the explosion point. Learn to identify your signals.

*Body signals*: How does your body feel when you are angry (sad, afraid, happy)? Are the muscles tense in your neck? arms, legs? Do you sweat or get cold? Do you breathe deeper, faster? lighter, slower? Do you get a headache, a stomachache?

*Behavioral signals*: How do you behave when you're feeling angry? Get mean? Blame others? Act extra nice? Start laughing? Become sarcastic? Withdraw? Break commitments? Arrive late or leave early? Have difficulty eating or sleeping? Eat or sleep more?

## TIME-OUTS

Time-outs are a basic tool for controlling violence. They provide a structure that allows you to break abusive patterns. Time-outs not only stop the violence, they also help to rebuild trust. The rules are simple:

- When you're angry say, "I'm beginning to feel angry. I need to take a time-out." In this way you communicate directly; you take responsibility for your own feelings and assure the other person that you're committed to avoiding violence.
- Leave for an hour.
- Don't take drugs or drive.
- Do something physical. Take a walk, run, ride a bike.

- Return in an hour (no more, no less). If you live up to your agreement, it will build trust.
- Ask the person you were angry with if he or she wants to discuss what made you angry.

Alcohol and drugs do not cause violence. But if you have a problem with violence they can make it worse. Alcohol and drugs may lessen your ability to control violent impulses.

Do you ever feel desperate during a time of battering and panic? Here are some things to do when you are feeling desperate.

1. Breathe deeply.
2. Get a favorite item of clothing or book and hold it.
3. Put on a relaxation tape.
4. Sit in your rocking chair.
5. Call a friend.
6. Call another friend if that friend is not at home.
7. Stroke your dog or cat.
8. Take a hot bath.
9. Write a hundred times, "I'm safe."
10. Run around the block three times.
11. Listen to soothing music.
12. Pray.
13. Breathe again.
14. Yell into your pillow.
15. Watch an old movie on TV or read a mystery novel.
16. Eat.
17. Start again at #1.

Sometimes you feel so bad about your parents and their problems that you want to die. The pain is so great, your feelings of self-loathing are so strong, the fear is so intense that you really don't want to live. These are real feelings, and it is important that you don't deny them. It is essential, however, that you do not act on them. It's okay to feel devastated. It's not okay to hurt yourself.

It is hardest to reach out when you need it the most, but give yourself a loving push to break out of your isolation. If you're with a true friend, you can ask to be hugged. If you're alone, call someone. It's a good idea to plan this before things with your parents get out of hand. Have several numbers close by to call if things get sticky at home, if the battering and abuse become more than you can stand.

If you are in a support group or in therapy, arrange to call the therapist or a group member. Make a contract with a friend that you'll call each other when you're in need. Making the call may be the last thing you feel like doing, but you have to honor the contract and your friend, so pick the phone up and DIAL.

Almost anything that works is fair in dealing with home abuse, but there are a few things you should avoid.

- Don't enter stressful or dangerous situations.
- Stay off the road.
- Don't drink or abuse drugs.
- Avoid making important decisions.
- Don't hurt youself or anyone else.

## SELF-DEFENSE FOR WOMEN

All women are targets of violence. Even if you use good judgment, have solid self-defense skills, and firmly believe you have the right to protect yourself, you are not immune to assault. For battering survivors, the risks are even greater.

A high percentage of women who were sexually abused as children have been revictimized in adulthood through assault, rape, and battering. When this happens, the adult frequently blames herself or feels that somehow she deserved it. This is false. She did not deserve it. The reason so many survivors experience violence as adults is that they were trained to be victims. The effects of childhood abuse leave them especially vulnerable.

If you are unable to identify your own feelings or gauge other people's intentions, you may not recognize danger. If you space out, you may not see the warning signs.

In order to feel comfortable around other people, especially men, you need to know you can protect yourself. The ability to say no firmly and to move out of a bad situation is enough to keep you safe.

Some abusive men, fathers, boyfriends are not stopped by words alone. Then you need to use more self-defense skills—shouting, yelling, kicking, hitting. Women in this society are not encouraged to be combative on their own behalf, but you have the right and responsibility to take care of yourself.

One practical and effective form of self-defense is called Model Mugging. Model Mugging is a fifteen- to twenty-hour course in which women do not just practice self-defense, they use full-force defense in simulated battering situations. The course is taught by a woman instructor and a man who is specifically trained to be a "model mugger."

The mugger wears protective gear. He attacks each woman in a realistic scenario, approaching her with obscene and insulting language. For the first time, women in this course are taught to deliver a knockout blow. Model Mugging is an intensive, effective way to move toward personal safety. Whether you use it or other forms of self-defense, learn to protect yourself and you will never be a victim of battering.

## ESCAPING FROM BATTERING

If you or your mother experience one of these signs, follow an escape plan and GET OUT. Has the abuser:

- pushed or shoved you?
- held you back to keep you from running?
- slapped, bitten, kicked, or choked you?
- hit or punched you?
- thrown objects at you?
- abandoned you in dangerous places?
- refused to help you when you were sick or injured?
- subjected you to reckless driving?
- threatened to hurt you with a weapon?

You're the only person who can decide how much is too much pain and what you are ready to do about it. You don't have to take suffering. Life can be good. Don't waste it on a sick person.

Amanda Stewart lived in a battering home growing up. Here is her story.

Life was very hard for me and my family. My father was a very sick man. To this day I still love him, but I cannot even go visit him in the rest home without remembering how he made our life a living hell for years.

I don't know when the trouble really started. I cannot remember a time when there wasn't some kind of trouble at our home, and I thought all homes were the same until I grew up and realized what I had been denied—a happy childhood and a safe home.

I don't know why Dad treated Mom so bad. Mom was a terrific person, always doing something for somebody else, always thinking of ways to make somebody's life simpler. And her own life was pure hell.

Dad didn't drink a lot, but boy, did he have a horrible temper. When he had a bad day at work, we all paid for it. He would storm into the house ranting and raving, flapping his hands this way and that. My brother and I ran for our rooms—we knew what was coming.

He started out just pushing Mom around—kidding. Then it got to the point where he liked pushing her around. He never tried to push me or my little brother around, I guess because he knew I would try to kill him.

After a couple of years it really got bad. Dad would start bopping Mom around first thing in the morning. Do you know how hard it is to wake up hearing your mother cry? I couldn't cry—I couldn't fall apart, I had my little brother to look after. He needed me, and in my own way I needed him to give me a reason to keep going. Well, Mom died of a heart attack four years ago. My brother is out of high school, and I'm married. Dad is living at a rest home. Life has gone on, but I will never forget those years.

## WHERE TO GET HELP

*Battered Wives*
Del Martin
Volcano Press, #518, Dept. B

330 Ellis Street
San Francisco, CA 94102

*Getting Free*
Ginny McCarthy
Seal Press
3131 Western Avenue, Suite 410
Seattle WA 98102-1028

*The Battered Woman*
Lenore Walker
Harper and Row, New York, 1979

CHAPTER ◊ 11

# Life at Home

## DAILY CHOICES

You make choices every day of your life. You make choices at school, with your friends, about what you wear, what you eat, what kind of person you become. Many of your major choices are the ones you make at home. Those choices will follow you the rest of your life, so they are very important.

Most of the daily choices you make at home have to do with your mom, dad, sisters, and brothers. Not only do you have to think about yourself, you have to consider your family members also.

The choices we shall discuss have to do with: discipline, curfews, chores, allowance, grades, getting along with teachers, choosing friends, when you have to work, and when you date. These are questions that many teenagers have to decide sooner or later.

When making a decision or a choice, do not hurry, and do not worry about what anyone else will think. Your decisions rest on your own individual life and family style of living. Every family is different and so are its choices.

## DISCIPLINE

Discipline is defined as training that teaches one to obey rules and control his behavior. What form of discipline do your parents use? Do you agree with it? Do you go by it? What happens if you don't obey the family rules? Every family is as different as makes of cars, so a rule that pertains to your family may not pertain to your friend's family.

It is a good idea to talk about your own family rules from time to time. If you do not agree with your parents' decisions, discuss them honestly. Between you and your parents you should be able to find some rules that you both agree on.

## CURFEW

What is a curfew? Most parents consider a curfew to be the time when their teenagers must be in from an evening out. Curfews vary just as families vary. If both of your parents work, you may need to be in earlier so that you won't disturb their sleep. If you have younger brothers and sisters, you may need to be in so as not to wake them up. Average curfews for teens across the United States for a week night are around 9:00 to 9:30. Curfews for the weekend go from 11:00 to midnight. What happens if you stay later than your curfew? What will your parents do? Do you think it is fair? If not, plan some time to discuss your feelings about your curfew. Most parents are willing to listen to what you have to say if you have thought about it beforehand. Don't pop off and yell. Keep your cool and be calm. Prove to your parents that you can act in an adult manner.

## CHORES

This is not a popular subject between teens and their parents, although it must be discussed. A major consideration in the matter of chores is whether your mother is working full time, part time, or not at all. Wealthy families have maid and cleaning services to take care of the house, but most families need their children to help keep things running smoothly. If you live with a working mother, most likely you will have more chores than your friend whose mother doesn't work. Don't resent it if your mother works; be glad that she cares enough to give you the best possible.

To help you and your family keep the chores straight, make up a daily schedule and post it where it can be seen by every family member. Here is an example of a chore schedule:

|  | M | T | W | TH | F |
|---|---|---|---|---|---|
| *Ted* | Wash | Cook | Errands | Yard | Free |
| *Kelli* | Cook | Wash | Yard | Free | Errands |

Every day of the week each family member has a different chore to do. One day can be a free day if you wish. Some parents include their names on the chore schedule. Chores vary from family to family. The chart helps each member know just what is expected daily. There is no guesswork or forgetting. Chores are different every day to reduce boredom, although no chore is considered fun.

## ALLOWANCE

Whether you receive an allowance or not is up to your parents, and not all parents feel that children should be paid. Many teens are rewarded for good report cards, but most are paid for chores, duties, and baby-sitting within the family.

Do you really need an allowance? What do you need one for? If you believe you deserve an allowance, by all means sit down and talk with your parents about it. If you feel you need more than what you receive now as an allowance, talk to your parents. Parents cannot always read your mind. Keep the lines of communication open.

## GRADES

If you could look down the road to your future and see how your grades reflected your attitude toward life and your goals, you would appreciate their importance. Grades are not only important in school, but they are essential to your basic self-esteem, how you handle yourself in different situations. Not all of us can be brilliant, but all of us can do the best work we are capable of.

## GETTING ALONG WITH TEACHERS

This is vital to every aspect of your life. Why? Why should you get along with your teachers? Because you should obey all adults and a teacher is an adult? No, you won't be in school the rest of your life, but most of you will have to earn a living, and you will have to get along with your boss. Some of you may be thinking you won't have to work. But even if you are out of school and not working, you will have a spouse to get along with. Getting along with teachers teaches you how to get along in life. You can bet there will be teachers you don't like, teachers who aren't fair. But so it is in life. You will have bosses you don't like, bosses who are not fair to you, but you have to keep going. Getting along with teachers is learning to get along with life.

## CHOOSING FRIENDS

It is impossible to overemphasize the importance of choosing friends carefully. The friends you choose carry into other parts of your life. In junior high and high school, friends play a huge role in your life. Never again will you lean so much on them and learn so much about life. Friends can bless your life and make the rough spots easier, or ruin your life and lead you down the wrong roads.

Your parents' opinions of your friends say a lot about their character. Your parents are older and wiser than you and have experience in judging people. They can see things you may not see. Listen to their opinions. Try not to block out what they are saying if you do not agree. They want only the best for you and your life.

If you like a particular friend of whom they don't approve, ask them why? Sit down and talk to your parents. Ask for their reasoning.

It is best to have friends of the same background as you, friends who have things in common with you. Remember, friends who want you to do things that you feel strongly against are not really friends. Friends who constantly get you into trouble are not friends. Ask yourself whether this one friend is worth a lot of heartache and worry with your family?

Real friends will be with you through good and bad times. You will find out who your true friends are when you go through a crisis; look around and see who is with you. Good friends should bring out the best in you, and you should bring out the best in them. Good friends try to get along with your parents, and encourage you to make good grades, and observe your curfew. Good friends will not lie to you or steal your boyfriend. A good friend will stand up for you when nobody else will. Good friends are worth their weight in gold. But to have a friend, you have to be a friend.

## WHEN YOU HAVE TO WORK

About 20 percent of American teenagers have to work, not just for extra things like clothes or trips, but to eat and have clothes at all. Is this a shame? Yes and no. It's sad that some teens miss out on activities such as band and orchestra, choir, and speech team because they work. And it is true that they miss a lot of studying time. But the things they learn by working are invaluable.

Working as a teenager gives you a better perspective of life. Working helps you to decide what you want to do when you graduate. Working helps you decide if a college education would be worth it or not.

Working at a variety of jobs helps you choose your career. What kind of career would you like? If you think you would like to be a teacher, work as a teacher's aide. If you would like to work around clothes, work at a dress store. What about working at the bank? The newspaper? As a secretary? Try working at the hospital as a volunteer. Work at a rest home, restaurant, park, telephone company, music company, day-care center, cafeteria, beauty shop, jewelry shop, photography lab, medical lab, insurance, television station, radio station, grocery store, florist, computer store, furniture store, eye doctor. Try as many different types of jobs as you can. As you get older you won't have so much opportunity to change jobs.

Working while in school is a good way to meet other teenagers, both girls and boys. It's not easy juggling school and job and social life, but it can be done.

Working while in school helps you learn the value of money. You learn quickly just how hard that dollar is to come by, and you respect it more.

## WHEN YOU DATE

Dating is one of the most enjoyable things about growing up. You can learn so much about yourself and life through the excitement of dating. You should know the answers to some questions before you start dating a person. Is he about your age and of the same kind of family? What kind of education is he getting, and what are his goals for the future? Do his religious beliefs agree with yours? What is his attitude toward life? How does he get along with your parents, and you with his? Do you have a lot in common or is it all physical attraction?

Many teens cannot tell the difference between physical attraction and love? How do you tell? In physical attraction the only thing you like about the person is looks; other than that you have nothing in common. In love you honestly care about the person. You put his needs and desires before your own.

How long should you date a person while you are still in school? It depends on you and that person. Many parents feel it is wrong for a teenager to be tied to the same person all through high school. That is a decision you will have to make. A lot of good marriages have started out in high school, but so have a lot of divorces. Remember, your entire future is before you. Don't hold onto one person just for fear of being alone.

Is it okay not to date in school? Yes. Some teens feel they just aren't ready for all that pressure. It's your life, and you don't have to keep up with anyone or worry about what anyone else thinks of you.

# Bibliography

Ackerman, Robert. *Children of Alcoholics*. New York: Simon & Schuster, Inc., 1983.

Bass, Ellen, and Davis, Laura. *The Courage to Heal*. New York: Harper & Row Publishers, 1988.

Beattie, Melody. *Codependent No More*. New York: Harper & Row Publishers, 1987.

Belli, Melvin, and Krantzler, Mel. *The Complete Guide for Men and Women Divorcing*. New York: St. Martin's Press, 1988.

Bradshaw, John. *The Family*. Deerfield Beach, Florida: Health Communications Inc., 1988.

Colgrave, Melba, and Bloomfield, Harold H. *How to Survive the Loss of a Love*. New York: Bantam Books, 1976.

Donnelly, Katherine. *Recovering from the Loss of a Sibling*. New York: Dodd, Mead & Company, 1988.

————. *Recovering from the Loss of a Parent*. New York: Dodd, Mead & Company, 1986.

————. *Recovering from the Loss of a Child*. New York: Dodd, Mead & Company, 1985.

Fensterheim, Robert. *Making It Right When It Feels All Wrong*. New York: Rawson Associates, 1988.

Kline, Nathan. *From Sad to Glad*. New York: Ballantine Books, 1987.

Krauss, Pesach. *Why Me?* New York: Bantam Books, 1988.

Kubler-Ross, Elisabeth. *AIDS—The Ultimate Challange*. New York: Macmillan Publishing, 1987.

Morra, Marion. *Choices*. New York: Avon Books, 1978.

Pinkham, Mary Ellen. *How to Keep Your Loved Ones from Drinking*. New York: G.P. Putnam and Sons, 1983.

Sunshine, Linda. *The 100 Best Treatment Centers for Alcoholism and Drug Abuse*. New York: Avon Books, 1988.

Swindoll, Charles. *Growing Wise in Family Life*. New York: Zondervan Publishing, 1988.

# Index